Elhanan Winchester

The Three Woe Trumpets

Of which the First and Second are Already Past...

Elhanan Winchester

The Three Woe Trumpets
Of which the First and Second are Already Past...

ISBN/EAN: 9783337102616

Printed in Europe, USA, Canada, Australia, Japan

Cover: Foto ©ninafisch / pixelio.de

More available books at **www.hansebooks.com**

THE

THREE WOE TRUMPETS;

OF WHICH

THE FIRST AND SECOND ARE ALREADY PAST:

AND

THE THIRD IS NOW BEGUN;

UNDER WHICH

THE SEVEN VIALS OF THE WRATH OF GOD ARE TO BE POURED OUT UPON THE WORLD.

BEING

THE SUBSTANCE OF TWO DISCOURSES,

FROM REV. xi. 14, 15, 16, 17, 18.

Delivered at the Chapel in Parliament Court, Artillery Street, Bishopsgate Street,

On FEBRUARY 3, *and* 24, 1793.

BY ELHANAN WINCHESTER,

THE SECOND EDITION.

LONDON:

Printed for and sold by SAMUEL R[illegible]o. 1, Carthusian Street, Aldersgate Street; by T. [illegible]ONS, No. 21, Paternoster Row; and by the AUTHOR, No. 5, Wink[illegible]worth's Buildings, City Road.

—

PRICE ONE SHILLING.

DISCOURSE I.

REVELATIONS xi. 14.

THE SECOND WOE IS PAST; AND BEHOLD THE THIRD WOE COMETH QUICKLY!

I THINK I may addreſs you as our Lord did his hearers upon another occaſion: "This day is "this Scripture fulfilled in your ears." Were I to ſearch the ſacred prophecies over from beginning to end, I could not find a paſſage more in ſeaſon than this. I am perſuaded that the *Second Woe* is now juſt paſt, and that the *Third Woe* cometh quickly, and will begin immediately to follow the concluſion of the Second.

In order to caſt what light I can upon this paſſage, I ſhall take notice in a brief manner of the Three WOE TRUMPETS: Two of which I believe are now finiſhed, and the Third juſt beginning to ſound. For though it is very evident that all the Trumpets brought great woes and deſtructions upon the Earth, yet the Fifth, Sixth, and Seventh, are by way of eminence called, the *Woe Trumpets*, as the destructions and miseries that have befallen, and shall befal mankind under them, are far greater, and of longer continuance than those under the first four. For after the four first angels had sounded, and very awful judgments and desolations had followed, which refer to events long since past and gone, St. John says, "And I beheld, and heard "an Angel flying through the midst of Heaven, "saying with a loud voice, Woe, woe, woe, to "the inhabiters of the earth, by reason of the "other voices of the trumpets of the three Angels "which are yet to sound." Chap. viii. 13.

We are naturally led from this proclamation to expect very awful woes and desolations to follow; and we shall not be disappointed.

Chap. ix. 1. 2. "And the fifth Angel sounded, "and I saw a Star fall from heaven unto the earth: "and to him was given the key of the bottomless pit. "And he opened the bottomless pit, and there "arose a smoke out of the pit, as the smoke of a "great furnace; and the sun and the air were dark-"ened, by reason of the smoke of the pit."

By this Star, I understand the impostor Mahomet, by whom a false religion was set up, which has had a very extensive spread, insomuch that it has filled a considerable part of the world with error and darkness; and which religion did not come down from heaven, but rose out of the bottomless pit, and has been extended by the agency of the angel of the bottomless pit, or the great destroyer of mankind. It seems astonishing, that a religion so false, senseless, and stupid, should have ever prevailed where Christianity in its purity had been known! But it was permitted by God, as a dreadful woe, to punish those Christians who had lost the truth, life,

and

and power of their religion, and had in a manner turned their light into darkneſs, and degenerated into mere idolators. And beſides, it was propagated by the ſword, without which it would never have been ſpread in the world at all. This falſe prophet is very aptly and juſtly typified by a blazing ſtar, or meteor, and his religion by ſmoke and darkneſs out of the bottomleſs pit, which darkened the ſun and the air.

Verſe 3. " And there came out of the ſmoke " Locuſts upon the earth; and unto them was " given power, as the ſcorpions of the earth have " power."

Moſt expoſitors agree that theſe locuſts repreſent the armies of the Saracens, who came forth with the doctrine of Mahomet in their mouths, and arms in their hands, to deſtroy the remains of the Chriſtian Faith, and to conquer the fineſt parts of the eaſtern empire. The Arabians are properly compared to locuſts, not only becauſe numerous armies are frequently compared to them, but alſo becauſe ſwarms of locuſts often ariſe from Arabia, and alſo becauſe in the plagues of Egypt, to which conſtant alluſion is made in theſe trumpets; the locuſts were brought by an eaſt wind, and came from Arabia, which lies eaſtward of Egypt: and alſo becauſe in the book of Judges the people of Arabia are compared to locuſts or graſshoppers for multitude. As the natural locuſts are bred in pits and holes of the earth, ſo theſe myſtical locuſts are truly infernal, and proceed with the darkneſs from the bottomleſs pit. " Theſe had power, as the " ſcorpions of the earth have power;"—a proper ſimilitude to expreſs their great power to deſtroy and torment mankind.

Verſe 4. " And it was commanded them that " they ſhould not hurt the graſs of the earth, nei- " ther any green thing, neither any tree; but only " thoſe men which have not the Seal of God in their " foreheads."

This plainly ſhews that they are not natural locuſts, which commonly feed upon graſs and green things, but figurative locuſts, which are rightly explained to mean the Arabians; to whom theſe orders were given, when they were marching to invade Syria, " Deſtroy no palm-trees, nor burn any " fields of corn: cut down no fruit-trees, nor do " any miſchief to cattle, only ſuch as you kill to " eat." Their commiſſion was to hurt only thoſe men who had not the ſeal of God in their foreheads; that is, thoſe who were not the true ſervants of God, but corrupt and idolatrous Chriſtians. Their wars were chiefly intended for the propagation of the Mahometan religion; their aim was not ſo much to hurt individuals in their property, as to eſtabliſh their principles among them, in oppoſition to a corrupted Chriſtianity that had taken place. And it appears evident from hiſtory, that in thoſe countries of Aſia, Africa, and Europe, where the Saracens extended their conqueſts, the Chriſtians were generally guilty of Idolatry, in worſhipping ſaints, if not images; and it was the pretence of Mahomet and his followers to chaſtiſe them for it, and to re-eſtabliſh the unity of the Godhead.

Verſe 5. " And to them it was given, that they " ſhould not kill them, but that they ſhould be tor- " mented five months; and their torment was as " the torment of a ſcorpion, when he ſtriketh a man."

Theſe Saracens, or Arabians, compared to Locuſts, were only to hurt thoſe men who had not the

the ſeal of God in their foreheads, and they were not commiſſioned to kill or wholly deſtroy them politically; but were allowed greatly to harraſs, diſtreſs, and torment them. And this was to be the caſe for five months, which time is twice repeated.

The five months are ſuppoſed to agree with the incurſions of the Saracens, in ſeveral reſpects. Firſt, It is in the five ſummer months, from May to September, that the Locuſts deſtroy the productions of the earth; ſo in theſe months the Saracens made their invaſions. Locuſts are obſerved to live about five months, viz. from April to September; and if we take theſe five months for natural months, then as the natural Locuſts live and do hurt only in the five ſummer months, ſo the Arabians made their excurſions in the five ſummer months, and retreated again in the winter. It appears that this was their uſual practice, and particularly when they firſt beſieged Conſtantinople, in the time of Conſtantine Pogonatus. For from the month of April until September, they pertinaciouſly continued their ſiege, and then deſpairing of ſucceſs, departed to Cyzicum, where they wintered, and in ſpring again renewed the war: and this courſe they held for ſeven years, as the Greek annals tells us.

Secondly, Some think that the time of five months is to be underſtood prophetically, for one hundred and fifty years; and it is very remarkable that within that time the Saracens made their principal conqueſts. Their empire might ſubſiſt much longer, but their power of hurting and tormenting men was exerted chiefly within that period. Read the hiſtory of the Saracens, and you will find their greateſt exploits were performed, and their greateſt conqueſts

conquests made, betweeen the year six hundred and twelve, when Mahomet first opened the bottomless pit, and began publickly to teach and propagate his imposture, and the year seven hundred and sixty two, when the Caliph Almansor, built Bagdat, to fix there the seat of his empire, and called it, THE CITY OF PEACE. Syria, Persia, India, and the greatest part of Asia; Egypt, and the greatest part of Africa; Spain, and some parts of Europe, were all subdued in the intermediate time.

Thirdly, If these months be taken doubly, for three hundred years, then according to Sir Isaac Newton in his Observations on the Revelations, "the whole time that the Caliphs of the Saracens "reigned with a temporal dominion at Damascus "and Bagdat together, was three hundred years; "viz. from the year six hundred and thirty-seven, "to the year nine hundred and thirty-six inclusive," when their empire was broken, and divided into several principalities or kingdoms. So that let these five months be taken in any possible construction, the event will still answer, and the prophecy be fulfilled; though perhaps the second method of interpretation and application is best.

Their torment being like the torment of a scorpion when he striketh a man, signifies, that as a scorpion puts a man to extreme pain and torture by piercing his natural body, so the Saracens tormented by piercing and wounding the political body oft he Roman empire.

Ver. 6. "And in those days shall men seek "death, and shall not find it; and shall desire to "die, and death shall flee from them."

The Saracen woe must have been great and terrible indeed, to cause men to wish for death, rather

ther than to ſee and feel the miſeries cauſed by their invaſions and irruptions; it would have been far more deſirable to the nations they harraſſed to have been made provinces of their empire, and thereby to have enjoyed peace, than to be continually tormented with their invaſions.

Verſe 7. "And the ſhapes of the locuſts were "like unto horſes prepared unto battle; and on "their heads were, as it were, crowns like gold, and "their faces were as the faces of men."

In this and ſeveral following verſes, the nature and qualities of theſe locuſts are deſcribed, partly in alluſion to the properties of natural locuſts, and the deſcription given of them by Joel the prophet, and partly in alluſion to the manners and cuſtoms of the Arabians, to ſhew that not real but figurative locuſts are here intended.

The firſt quality mentioned is their being *like unto horſes* prepared unto the battle; which is copied from Joel ii. 4. "The appearance of them (the locuſts) "is as the appearance of horſes, and as horſemen ſo "ſhall they run." Many authors have obſerved that the head of a locuſt reſembles that of an horſe. The Italians therefore, call them *Cavalette*, as it were little horſes. It is a ſtriking and beautiful repreſentation of the ſwiftneſs and expedition with which an army conſiſting of horſemen, invade and ravage a country. The Arabians have in all ages been famous for their horſes and horſemanſhip; their ſtrength is well known to conſiſt chiefly in their cavalry.

Another diſtinguiſhing mark and character, is their having *on their heads, as it were, crowns like gold;* which ſeems to be an alluſion to the head-dreſs of the Arabians, who have conſtantly worn turbans or mitres, and boaſt of having thoſe ornaments in

their

their common attire, which are crowns and diadems with other people. The crowns may alfo fignify the kingdoms and dominions which they fhould acquire: For, as Mr. MEDE excellently obferves, " No nation had ever fo wide a command;
" nor ever were fo many kingdoms, fo many re-
" gions fubjugated in fo fhort a fpace of time. It
" founds incredible, yet moft true it is, that in the
" fpace of eighty, or not many more years, they
" fubdued and acquired to the diabolical empire of
" Mahomet, Paleftine, Syria, both Armenias, al-
" moft all Afia Minor, Perfia, India, Egypt, Nu-
" midia; all Barbary, even to the river Niger;
" Portugal, Spain. Neither did their fortune or
" ambition ftop here, till they had added alfo a
" great part of Italy, as far as to the gates of Rome;
" moreover, Sicily, Candia, Cyprus, and the other
" ifles of the Mediterranean fea. How great a tract
" of land! how many *crowns* are here! Whence
" alfo it is worthy of obfervation, that mention is
" not made here, as in other trumpets, *of the third*
" *part*; forafmuch as this plague fell no lefs with-
" out the bounds of the Roman empire than with-
" in it, and extended itfelf even to the remoteft
" Indies."

Their faces being *like the faces of men*, fhews them not to be real, but only figurative locufts: and it is faid that the Arabians wore their beards, or at leaft muftachoes, which gave them a manly appearance; and poffibly their faces being like men, may intend their pretences of ufing reafon and arguments like men, in order to fpread and propagate their religion in the world.

Verfe 8. " And they had hair as the hair of
" women, and their teeth were as the teeth of
" lions."

Though

Though they wore long muſtachoes to make themſelves appear like men, yet they wore long hair, dreſſed and plaited, or flowing like that of women. This was the cuſtom of the Arabians, as ſeveral authors teſtify, and is another proof that natural locuſts cannot be intended, but the Saracens, who are all along deſcribed in this viſion. Their effeminacy and luſt, to which they were extremely addicted, are hinted at here, as well as their manner of dreſs and attire. *Their teeth as the teeth of lions*, is a deſcription copied from Joel's prophecy reſpecting the natural locuſts, " A nation, whoſe teeth are " the teeth of a lion, and he hath the cheek teeth " of a great lion :" Joel i. 6. that is, ſtrong to devour; and it is wonderful to obſerve with what rapaciouſneſs the natural locuſts bite and devour all before them, and gnaw, as Pliny ſays, even the doors of houſes. And how amazingly ſtrong the Arabians were, like lions, to devour and eat up the riches of the people, during the time that God permitted them to ravage and deſtroy the countries!

Verſe 9. " And they had breaſt-plates, as it were " breaſt-plates of iron; and the ſound of their " wings was as the ſound of chariots of many horſes " running to battle."

There ſeems in this deſcription of the figurative locuſts, or Arabians, conſtant alluſions to the Prophet Joel's deſcription of the natural locuſts, as any one may perceive that compares them together. In chap. ii. verſe 8. ſpeaking of the locuſts, he ſays, " When they fall upon the ſword they ſhall not be " wounded." And it is obſervable, that the natural locuſt hath about its body a pretty hard ſhell, of the colour of iron; ſo that herein the ſymbol of the breaſt-plate is exactly ſuited to the natural locuſt. This metaphor is deſigned to expreſs the defenſive arms of the Saracens, as *the teeth of lions* was deſigned to expreſs their offenſive and deſtroying weapons.

Joel alſo deſcribes the natural locuſts in their march, in much the ſame language as St. John here uſes: Joel ii. 4, 5. "The appearance of them is as the "appearance of horſes; and as horſemen ſo ſhall "they run. Like the noiſe of chariots on the tops "of mountains ſhall they leap, like the noiſe of a "flame of fire that devoureth the ſtubble, as a "ſtrong people ſet in battle array."

The locuſts when they come in large bodies make ſuch a noiſe with their wings, that they might almoſt be taken for birds. *Their wings, and the ſound of their wings*, denote the ſwiftneſs and rapidity of their conqueſts; and it is indeed aſtoniſhing, that in leſs than a century they erected an empire, which extended from India to Spain. They not only conquered and poſſeſſed all Spain, except a few inacceſſible places in the mountains which they deſpiſed, but they paſſed over the Pyrenean mountains into France; and after many ravages in ſeveral parts of the country, they came to a deciſive battle with Charles Martel, in which *Aldirachman* was killed, with his numerous army. They advanced, as to a certain victory, with their wives and children, as deſigning to dwell in France; their army conſiſted of about four hundred thouſand; and there was fought one of the moſt bloody battles, and moſt obſtinate fights that the world ever beheld. The ſlaughter was almoſt incredible; three hundred and ſeventy thouſand were killed. This was about the year 734; and if this battle had not put a ſtop to

their

their progreſs, they in all probability would ſoon have conquered Europe, and poſſeſſed the whole Chriſtian world, ſo called. But after this defeat the Saracens or Moors made no farther conqueſts in Europe, and were afterwards quite driven out of Spain alſo. France, in that inſtance, ſtood as the great rampart of Chriſtianity, by preventing theſe locuſts of the bottomleſs pit from overſpreading all the earth.

Verſe 10. "And they had tails like unto ſcor-
"pions, and they had ſtings in their tails; and
"their power was to hurt men five months."

Theſe Arabians are thrice in this deſcription compared to ſcorpions; verſes 3, 5, 10. "*Unto them* "*was given power, as the ſcorpions of the earth have* "*power; and their torment was as the torment of a* "*ſcorpion when he ſtriketh a man; and they had tails* "*like unto ſcorpions, and there were ſtings in their* "*tails,*" &c. Theſe expreſſions ſhew that they were hurtful and very miſchievous, and exceedingly tormented mankind; and not only ſo, but they drew a poiſonous train after them, and wherever they carried their arms, there alſo they diſtilled the venom of a falſe religion; thereby doing more eſſential injury to the ſouls of men, than ſcorpions could do to their bodies. Their invaſions cauſed great pain, uneaſineſs and torment wherever they came, ſo as to make men wiſh for death; and they carried with them the poiſon of error and deluſion, which has ever ſince prevailed over many millions of the human race; and they not only deſtroyed learning and knowledge, but in a great meaſure put out or obſcured the light of the goſpel, by their darkneſs, through all the eaſt countries, where it had ſhone with the greateſt ſplendor. We muſt not ſuppoſe that they did not kill or destroy multitudes of men, as individuals, but they did not overthrow or totally destroy the kingdoms of the earth, or the eastern part of the Roman empire; that was reserved for another power, as we shall see presently; but they continued for a certain time to hurt, distress, torment, and almost to ruin the several kingdoms and states into which they made their inroads.

Ver. 11. "And they had a king over them, "which is the angel of the bottomless pit, "whose name in the Hebrew tongue is Abaddon, "but in the Greek tongue hath his name Apol-"lyon."

It is an observation of Agur, "The locusts have "no king, yet go they forth all of them by bands;" Prov. xxx. 27. Though the natural locusts have no king, yet these figurative locusts have one, who is called, *the angel of the bottomless pit*, whose name in both Hebrew and Greek signifies *a destroyer*. This might seem to intimate that Satan, or the Devil himself, was by way of eminence the king or leader of the Saracens, and the prime author of their religion and government: and there is no doubt but he had a principal hand in the matter, and that they were under his influence, and devoted to his service, and they seem to have been inspired with his spirit. But Bishop Newton, and some others, think that Mahomet himself is intended; the following are his words: "It is farther "added, that *they had a king over them*: The same "person should exercise temporal as well as spiritual "sovereignty over them; and the Caliphs were "their emperors, as well as the heads of their re-"ligion. The king is the same as the *star* or *angel* "*of the bottomless pit*, whose name is *Abaddon* in "Hebrew, and *Apollyon* in Greek, that is, the *de-*

"*stroyer*.

" *ſtroyer*. Mr. MEDE imagines, that this is ſome allu-
" ſion to the name of *Obodas* the common names of
" the kings of that part of Arabia from whence Ma-
" homet came, as *Pharaoh* was the common name of
" the kings of Egypt, and *Cæſar* of the emperors
" of Rome: and ſuch alluſions are not unuſual in
" the ſtile of Scripture. However that be, the name
" agrees perfectly well with Mahomet and the Ca-
" liphs his ſucceſſors, who were the authors of all
" thoſe horrid wars and deſolations, and openly
" taught and profeſſed that their religion was to
" be propagated and eſtabliſhed by the ſword. *"

Verſe

* It may, perhaps, be agreeable to the younger part of my readers, to give here a ſhort account of this Leader or King of the Saracens, out of Prideaux's Life of Mahomet.

" About the year of Chriſt 606, *Mahomet* began to pretend to Revelation, and converſe with the Angel *Gabriel*, in a ſolitary cave, near *Mecca*, in *Arabia*.

" In the year 608, which was the fortieth of his age, he began to take the ſtile of the Apoſtle of God; and to propagate his impoſture, he pretended not to deliver a new religion, but to revive the old religion God firſt gave to Adam: and by many other ſpecious pretences of receiving his Revelations from the angel Gabriel, he gained ſeveral proſelytes. Yet the people of *Mecca*, where he lived, were ſo averſe to his impoſture, that they reſolved to ſtrike at the root, and prevent the ſpreading of farther miſchief, by cutting him off who was the chief author of it; ſo that he was forced to fly from *Mecca* to *Medina*, then called *Yathreb*. This was in the year 622, from which flight of Mahomet, the *Hegira*, or computation of Time among the Mahometans, begins.

" From

Verse 12. " One woe is past, and behold there " come two woes more hereafter."

I trust.

" From this time he tells his disciples, his religion was not to be propagated by *disputing*, but by *fighting*.

" Accordingly the next year, 623, he fell upon the traders of *Mecca*, though guarded by a thousand men, and beat them; and spent the rest of the year in robbing, plundering, and destroying all those who would not come in to him, and embrace his religion.

" The next year he continued the same course, and fought a battle with a larger number of his opposers, in which he was overborne, and himself grievously wounded. To prevent the ill effects this disgrace might have on the minds of his followers, he taught them, that the time of life being determined by God, they who should be slain in battle, died no sooner than they must otherwise have done; and as they died fighting for the faith, they gained the crown of Martyrdom, and the rewards of Paradise.

" In the year 627, he was attacked by an army of ten thousand men, from which danger he very dexterously extricated himself; and the same year was inaugurated in the supreme authority, and made Head in all things civil and religious.

" In the year 629 Mahomet had an army of ten thousand men; so that he very soon brought most parts of *Arabia* into his power.

" In the year 630 he turned his arms towards *Syria*. In the year 631, all the *Arabs* came in, and submitted to him; and in the following year 632, he himself died, being 63 years of age, by the Arabian account, which make only 61 of ours. So that Mahomet within the space of twenty-four years, founded a new religion, and a new empire, throughout the large country of *Arabia*, a country bigger

than

I truſt it is very evident, by what has been obſerved from the foregoing verſes, that the riſe, progreſs, and conqueſts of Mahomet and his ſucceſſors, and the ravages of the Arabians, may properly be called *the firſt woe*; as it was indeed a moſt dreadful woe to the Chriſtian world ſo called, and to the inhabitants of all the countries where they committed their depredations.

The ſimilitude between the *Locuſts* and the Arabians is ſo great, that it muſt ſtrike every curious obſerver; and a farther reſemblance is noted by Mr. Daubuz: that "There hath happened in the extent of this torment, a coincidence of the event "with the nature of the locuſts. The Saracens "have made inroads into all thoſe parts of Chriſtendom where the natural locuſts are wont to be "ſeen and known to do miſchief, and no where elſe; "and that too in the ſame proportion. Where the "locuſts are ſeldom ſeen, there the Saracens ſtaid "little: where the natural locuſts are often ſeen, "there

than *Germany*, *Italy*, *Spain*, *France*, *Great Britain*, and *Ireland* together. Which, ſays Dr. Prideaux, "God has "permitted, in his all-wiſe Providence, to continue a "ſcourge unto us Chriſtians, who having received ſo holy "and ſo excellent a religion, through his mercy towards "us in Chriſt Jeſus our Lord, will not conform ourſelves "to live worthy of it."

It is indeed a moſt aſtoniſhing event, that this one man ſhould have riſen from nothing, in ſo ſhort a time, to ſuch great power, authority, and dominion; and that the impoſture which he propagated for religion ſhould have continued already for almoſt twelve hundred years, and during that time ſhould have as many profeſſed adherents as Chriſtianity itſelf, if not more! But I hope this will not remain the caſe much longer.

" there the Saracens abode moſt; and where they " breed moſt, there the Saracens had their begin- " ning and greateſt power. This may be eaſily veri- " fied by hiſtory."

The ſudden invaſion of the Saracens, the ſwift and almoſt incredible progreſs of their arms, many circumſtances peculiar to this people, and their invaſions, which ſufficiently diſtinguiſh them from all the invaſions of the northern nations, very properly anſwer the prophetic deſcription of theſe locuſts out of the bottomleſs pit. And the amazing miſeries which they cauſed wherever they came, ſlaying many, carrying many others captive, ſeizing the ſpoils and treaſures of the countries, deſtroying libraries, the repoſitories of learning; abuſing women, ſubjecting them to their brutal luſts, and eſpecially propagating a falſe religion in the world; all theſe things proved them to be the firſt terrible woe, which took place under the ſounding of the fifth Trumpet. This woe is paſt long ago, and I ſhould not have noticed it ſo particularly, but in order to throw light upon the ſubject I am about to treat of, viz. the concluſion of the ſecond woe. At the end of the firſt woe it is ſaid, *One woe is paſt, and behold there come two woes more hereafter.* This is added not only to diſtinguiſh the woes, and to mark more ſtrongly each period, but alſo to ſuggeſt that ſome time would intervene between this firſt woe, of the Arabian locuſts, and the next of the Euphratean horſemen.

We now paſs to notice, briefly, the *Second Woe*; which begun with ſounding the Sixth Trumpet, and is juſt now ended. And though I cannot ſpeak of all the events that have taken place under the ſound of the Sixth Trumpet, in this diſcourſe, yet

it

it will be a ſatisfaction if I ſhould be able to point out with certainty any event that was to take place at the beginning of the Second Woe, and another that was to cloſe it, and ſhew them both to be paſt; then it will appear evident to all, that the Second Woe is both begun and finiſhed. I know of no better way to expreſs my thoughts, than to read the prophetic deſcription, and then ſet down the hiſtoric account.

Verſes 13. 14. "And the ſixth angel ſounded, "and I heard a voice from the four horns of the "golden altar, which is before God, ſaying to "the ſixth Angel, who had the Trumpet, Looſe "the four angels which are bound in the great ri- "ver Euphrates."

Another dreadful plague, or woe, was about to come upon the world, as a puniſhment for their ſins; and therefore a voice was heard from the four horns of the golden altar, ordering the angel to looſe four deſtroying angels, to deſtroy mankind. Such a voice *proceeding* from *the golden altar*, is a ſtrong indication of the divine diſpleaſure; and plainly ſhews the ſins of men muſt be very great, when the altar which ſhould have been their ſanctuary and protection, called aloud for vengeance upon them.

I take theſe four angels to be the four ſultanies, or four leaders of the Turks and Othmans. For there were four principal ſultanies, or kingdoms, of the Turks, bordering upon the river Euphrates. One at Bagdad, founded by Togrul Beg, or Tangrolipix, as he is commonly called, in the year 1055 another at Damaſcus, founded by Tagjuddaulus, or Ducas, in the year 1079: a third founded by Sjarfuddaulus, or Melech, in the ſame year 1079: and the fourth at Iconium, in Aſia Minor, founded by

Sedyduddaulas or Cutlu Muſes, or his ſon, in the year 1080.

Theſe four Sultanies ſubſiſted ſeveral years afterwards; and the Sultans were *bound* and reſtrained from extending their conqueſts farther than the territories and countries adjoining to the river Euphrates, primarily by the Providence of God, and in a ſecondary ſenſe by the Croiſades or expeditions of the European Chriſtians into the holy land, in the latter part of the eleventh, and in the twelfth and thirteenth centuries. Nay, the European Chriſtians took ſeveral cities and countries from them, and confined them within narrower bounds. But when an end was put to the Croiſades, and the Chriſtians totally abandoned their conqueſts in Syria and Paleſtine, as they did in the latter part of the thirteenth century; then the four angels were looſed that had been before bound in or near the great river Euphrates.

Soliman Shah, the firſt Chief and founder of the Othman race, retreating with his three ſons from Jingiz Chan, and the Tartars, would have paſſed the river Euphrates, but was drowned, the time of *looſing the four angels* being not yet come. Diſcouraged at this accident, two of his ſons returned to their former habitations; but Ortogrul the third, with his three ſons Condoz, Sarubani, and Othman, remained ſome time in thoſe parts, and having obtained leave of Aladin, Sultan of Iconium, he came with four hundred of his Turks, and ſettled in the mountains of Armenia. From thence they began their excurſions; and the other Turks aſſociating with them, and following their ſtandard, they gained ſeveral victories over the Tartars on one ſide, and over the Chriſtians on the other.

Ortogrul died in the year 1288, and Othman his

his ſon ſucceeded him in power and authority; and in the year 1299, as ſome ſay, with the conſent of Aladin himſelf, he was proclaimed Sultan, and the founder of a new empire: and the people afterwards, as well as the new empire, were called by his name. For though they diſclaim the name of *Turks*, and aſſume that of *Othmans*, yet it is certain that they are a mixt multitude, the remains of the four Sultanies above mentioned, as well as the deſcendants of the houſe of Othman.

Verſe 15. "And the four angels were looſed, "which were prepared for an hour and a day, and "a month and a year, for to ſlay the third part of "men."

In this manner, and at this time *the four angels were looſed, which were prepared for an hour, and a day, and a month, and a year, to ſlay the third part of men.* I reckon them to be looſed from the time of Ortogrul, who begun to encroach upon the Chriſtians, and who laid the foundation of the preſent Turkiſh empire. The Turks, or Othmans were certainly prepared, for a ſeaſon, not only to torment, but *to ſlay the third part of men;* that is, the men of the Roman empire, and eſpecially in Europe, the third part of the world. The Latin, or Weſtern empire, was broken to pieces under the four firſt Trumpets; the Greek or eaſtern empire, was cruelly *hurt* and *tormented* under the fifth Trumpet; and it is predicted that under the ſixth trumpet it is to be *ſlain* and utterly deſtroyed. Accordingly all Aſia Minor, Syria, Paleſtine, Egypt, Thrace, Macedon, and all the countries which belonged to the Greek or Eaſtern Cæſars, the Othmans have conquered and ſubjected to their dominions. And they at preſent have one of the largeſt empires in the world, and poſſeſs the moſt lovely parts of the

 globe;

globe; almoſt all the countries that are mentioned in the Scriptures belong to them at this time; yea, the Holy Land itſelf, of which we read ſo much in the Bible, forms but a very ſmall and diminutive part of their dominion.

They firſt paſſed over into Europe in the year 1357, in the reign of Orchan, their ſecond emperor. They took Conſtantinople, the capital of the Eaſtern empire, May 29th, 1453, in the reign of Mahomet their ſeventh emperor. Then they ſlew Conſtantine Paleologus the laſt Greek emperor, and put an end to that empire, which had ſubſiſted from the time of Conſtantine the Great. And in time all the remaining part of the Greek empire ſhared the fate of the capital city.

The laſt of their conqueſts was Candia, or ancient Crete, in the year 1669, and Cameniac, in the year 1672.

We may reckon the Turks as the greateſt deſtroyers of the human race that were ever raiſed up; and therefore they are ſaid to be prepared to ſlay the third part of men; and it is likely that in the courſe of their wars they may have actually ſlain as many perſons as would amount to nearly one third of all the people now living upon the earth. The expreſſion, *the third part of men*, may not be intended to convey the idea of exactly one third of men, but may chiefly be deſigned to ſignify many, or a conſiderable part of the whole; and to deſtroy the third part of men will then intend, that the deſtroying armies, now looſed from the river Euphrates, which had been one of the great boundaries of the empire, ſhould take away the lives of a great number of perſons, whoſe coun-

countries they ſhould on this permiſſion invade and conquer.

For the execution of this great work, it is ſaid that they were prepared for *an hour, and a day, and a month, and a year*; which will admit either of a literal or a myſtical interpretation; and the former will hold good, if the latter ſhould fail. If it be taken literally, it is only expreſſing the ſame thing by different words, as *peoples, and multitudes, and nations, and tongues*, are jointly uſed in other places; and then the meaning is, that they were prepared and ready to execute the divine commiſſion at any time, or for any time, any *hour*, or *day*, or *month*, or *year*, that God ſhould appoint. If it be taken myſtically, and the *hour* and *day*, and *month*, and *year*, be a prophetic *hour*, and *day*, and *month*, and *year*, then a *year* (according to St. John's computation, who follows that of Daniel) conſiſting of three hundred and ſixty days, is three hundred and ſixty years; and a *month* conſiſting of thirty days is thirty years; and a *day* is a year; and an *hour*, in the ſame proportion is fifteen days. So that the whole period of the Othmans *ſlaying the third part of men*, or ſubduing the Chriſtian States, in the Greek or Roman empire, amounts to three hundred and ninety-one years and fifteen days.

Now it is wonderfully remarkable, that the firſt conqueſt of the Othmans over the Chriſtians, was in the year of the Hegira, 680, and in the year of Chriſt 1281. For Ortogrul, in that year, (according to the accurate hiſtorian Saadi) crowned his victories with the conqueſt of the famous city Kutahi, from the Greeks:—Compute three hundred and ninety-one years from that time, and they will terminate in the year 1672; and, in that year Mahomet

homet the fourth took Cameniac from the Poles, and forty-eight towns and villages in the territory of Cameniac were delivered up to the Sultan, upon the treaty of peace. Whereupon Prince Cantemir hath made this memorable reflection, "This was "the last victory by which any advantage accrued "to the Othman state, or any city or province "was annexed to the ancient bounds of the em-"pire."

Other wars and slaughters have since taken place. The Turks even besieged Vienna in the year 1683; but this exceeding their commission, they were defeated. Belgrade, and other places have been taken from them, and surrendered to them again; but still they have subdued no new state or potentate of Christendom, for the space of an hundred and twenty years past; but on the contrary, the Russians of late, within that time, have taken part of their dominions from them; and it is likely will diminish them more and more.

Here then the prophecy and the event agree exactly in the period of three hundred and ninety-one years; and if we had more accurate and authentic histories of the Othmans, and knew the very day on which Kutahi was taken, as certainly as we may know that wherein Cameniac was taken, the like exactness would doubtless be found in the fifteen days.

But though the time be limited for the Othmans slaying *the third part of men*, yet no time is fixed for the duration of their empire. I am persuaded that they will be the principal leaders in the army that shall come against the children of Israel, after their return to their own land, and shall be destroyed at the coming of the Lord, as mentioned by the Prophets Ezekiel and Zachariah.

But

But as the ending of the *first woe* did not mean that the Arabians should be wholly destroyed, but only that their time of hurting men should be past; so also the ending of the *second woe* does not intend the total destruction of the Turkish empire, but only that their time of destroying *the third part of men* is at an end.

Verse 16. " And the number of the army of the " horsemen were two hundred thousand thousand: " and I heard the number of them."

The Turks are well known to be very numerous, and to have large bodies of cavalry; but the amazing number of two hundred million, or *myriads of myriads*, cannot be supposed to be brought into the field at once; as all the men upon the earth would scarcely amount to such a number; but we may easily suppose that from their first rise to their final overthrow, they may produce such a number of fighting men in all. And altho' they cannot all be on earth at once, but in succession, yet St. John could hear their numbers at once, as they were known to him who gave the Revelation to that beloved Apostle.

It is likely that this was nearly their combined sum in round numbers, as St. John particularly says, *And I heard the number of them*. Or it may be used to express their immense and innumerable multitudes, without being designed to set forth their exact number. The Othman Emperors have often brought very large armies into the field. When Mahomet the Second besieged Constantinople, he had about four hundred thousand men in his army, besides a powerful fleet of thirty large, and two hundred smaller ships. And often, in their wars with the Christian powers, they have brought prodigious hosts into the field, chiefly of horsemen. The

Ti-

Timariots, or horſemen holding lands by ſerving in the wars, are even at preſent the ſtrength of the government; and ſome ſay theſe are about a million of fighting men. And beſides theſe there are Spahi's, and other horſemen in the Emperor's pay.

Ver. 17. "And thus I ſaw the horſes in the viſion, "and them that ſat on them, having breaſt-plates "of fire, and of jacinct, and brimſtone: and the "heads of the horſes were as the heads of lions; "and out of their mouths iſſued fire, and ſmoke, and "brimſtone."

In the viſion, the riders upon theſe horſes, appeared to have breaſt-plates of fire and jacinct, and brimſtone. The colour of *fire* is red, of *jacinct* or hyacinth blue, and of *brimſtone* yellow: and this as Mr. Daubuz obſerves, "hath a literal accompliſhment; for the Othmans, from the firſt time of "their appearance, have affected to wear ſuch war-"like apparel of ſcarlet, blue, and yellow." Of the Spahi's, particularly, ſome have red, and ſome have yellow ſtandards, and others red or yellow, mixed with other colours.

The appearance of *the heads of the horſes were as the heads of lions*, to denote their ſtrength, courage and fierceneſs; and it appeared to the apoſtle in the viſion as though *fire and ſmoke, and brimſtone iſſued out of their mouths*. A manifeſt alluſion to gunpowder and great guns; which were invented under the Sixth Trumpet, and were of ſingular ſervice to the Othmans in their wars. St. John had never ſeen gun powder, nor artillery, but he almoſt deſcribes the compoſition of gun-powder, *fire, ſmoke*, and *brimſtone*; and the appearance of the diſcharge of fire-arms from men on horſeback; which

at

at a diſtance ſeems like fire, and ſmoke and brimſtone, coming out of the horſes mouths.

Verſe 18. " By theſe three was the third part of " men killed; by the fire, and by the ſmoke, and " by the brimſtone, which iſſued out of their " mouths."

By the uſe of gunpowder and great guns, the Othmans made great havoc and deſtruction in the Eaſtern empire. Amurath the Second broke into Peloponneſus, and took ſeveral ſtrong places by the means of his artillery. But his ſon Mahomet employed ſuch great guns as had never been uſed before. One is deſcribed to be of ſuch a monſtrous ſize, that it was drawn by ſeventy yoke of oxen, and by two thouſand men. There were two more, each of which diſcharged a ſtone, of the weight of two talents. Others emitted a ſtone of the weight of half a talent: But the greateſt of all diſcharged a ball of the weight of three talents, or about three hundred pounds; and the report of this cannon is ſaid to have been ſo great, that all the country round about was ſhaken to the diſtance of forty furlongs. For forty days the wall was battered by theſe guns, and ſo many breaches were made, that the city was taken by aſſault, and an end put to the Grecian or Eaſtern empire.

Now is it not wonderful that St. John ſhould have beheld in viſion this new way of deſtroying men, and taking cities, by the force of gunpowder, ſo different from all the methods that had ever been uſed in his time, or for many ages afterwards, even until the Turkiſh empire aroſe? But the ſame kind of inſtruments of deſtruction are now uſed by almoſt all nations.

Verſe 19. " For their power is in their mouth, " and in their tails; for their tails were like unto

" ſerpents, and had heads, and with them they do
" hurt."

The Turkiſh army of horſemen, carried deſtruction before and behind; the diſcharge of their artillery might appear to St. John as coming from the tails of their horſes, as well as fire and ſmoke and brimſtone from their mouths. But I rather think, with Biſhop Newton, that their tails being *like unto ſerpents*, and having *heads* with which *they do hurt*, intend their likeneſs to the Saracens, only the different tails are accommodated to the different creatures, the tails of *ſcorpions* to *locuſts*; the *tails* of *ſerpents* with *heads*, to *horſes*.—" By this figure " it is meant, that the Turks draw after them " the ſame poiſonous train as the Saracens; they " profeſs and propagate the ſame impoſture; they " do hurt, not only with their conqueſts, but alſo " by ſpreading their falſe doctrine; and wherever " they eſtabliſh their dominion, there too they eſta- " bliſh their religion. Many indeed of the Greek " Church remained, and are ſtill remaining among " them: but they are made to pay dearly for the " exercife of their religion; are ſubjected to a ca- " pitation-tax, which is rigorouſly exacted from " all above fourteen years of age; are burdened be- " ſides, with the moſt heavy and arbitrary impoſi- " tions upon every occaſion; are compelled to the " loweſt and moſt ſervile drudgery; are abuſed in " their perſons, and robbed of their property; have " not only the mortification of ſeeing ſome of their " friends and kindred daily apoſtatize to the ruling " religion, but have even their children taken from " them to be educated therein, of whom the more " robuſt and hardy are trained up to the ſoldiery, the " more weakly and tender are made eunuchs for the " ſeraglio. But notwithſtanding theſe perſecutions and

" op-

"oppressions, some remains of the Greek Church are
"still preserved among them, as we may reasonably
"conclude, to serve some great and mysterious ends
"of Providence."

I trust it has been made apparent that the *Saracens* were the first woe, under the Fifth Trumpet, and the *Turks* the second woe, under the Sixth Trumpet; which Trumpet has just now finished sounding; and the second woe is past, as I shall endeavour to prove.

Verse 20, 21. "And the rest of the men which
"were not killed by these plagues, yet repented
"not of the works of their hands, that they should
"not worship devils, and idols of gold, and silver,
"and brass, and stone, and of wood: which neither can see, nor hear, nor walk: Neither repented they of their murders, nor of their sorceries, nor of their fornication, nor of their thefts."

It was a dreadful judgment, which befel the Eastern Churches for their idolatries in worshipping saints, that the Saracens were permitted to chastise and torment them; but this plague working no reformation in them, they were again chastised by the still greater plague of the Othmans; were partly overthrown by the former, and were entirely ruined by the latter. But though the Eastern churches were ruined and destroyed by these plagues, yet the Western churches, who pretty well escaped these calamities, were not at all reclaimed, but still persisted in the worship of saints, or demons, the souls of dead men, and what is worse, the worship of images, *which neither can see, nor hear, nor walk*; and the world is witness to the completion of this prophecy to this day. *Neither repented they of their murders*, their persecutions and inquisitions; *nor of their sorceries*, their pretended miracles and revelations; nor of their fornication, their public ſtews and abominable uncleanneſs, for which they are noted; *nor of their thefts*, their exactions and impoſitions upon mankind: and they are as notorious for their licentiouſneſs and wickedneſs, as for their ſuperſtition and idolatry. They have refuſed to take warning by the two former woes, and therefore the third woe will fall upon them with all its force, and which is now immediately to commence. For,

"THE SECOND WOE IS PAST, AND BEHOLD, THE "THIRD WOE COMETH QUICKLY."

It cannot be expected that I ſhould take notice of all the events that have fallen under the ſound of the Sixth Trumpet: but I have noticed what events took place at the beginning, and muſt now, agreeable to my deſign, notice an event, which plainly ſhews that ſcene to be at an end; the ſecond woe to be paſt; and the Sixth Trumpet to have done ſounding. But before I come to ſpeak directly to this, I ſhall notice a verſe or two in the tenth chapter of this prophecy, in the oath of the angel, who ſet his right foot upon the ſea, and his left on the earth, and lifted up his hand to heaven, "And "ſware by him that liveth for ever and ever, who "created heaven, and the things that therein are, "and the earth, and the things that therein are, "and the ſea, and the things which are therein, that "there ſhould be time no longer." (or that the time ſhall not be yet, or that the glorious ſtate of the church, which God hath promiſed, ſhall not take place under the ſound of the ſixth trumpet.) "But "in the days of the voice of the ſeventh angel, when "he ſhall begin to ſound, (there ſhall no longer be any delay of time, but) "the myſtery of God ſhould

"be

" be finiſhed, as he hath declared to his ſervants the " prophets." Rev. x. 6, 7.

Theſe words have been ſtrangely miſunderſtood by ſome, as though the angel ſwore that there ſhould be an immediate end of time, and that it referred to the laſt judgment, and deſtruction of the world. But this is evidently contrary to common ſenſe; the plain meaning, according to ſeveral judicious interpreters, is what I have mentioned above. Mr. Lowman thus paraphraſes on the words, " But though I was not allowed to reveal what the " ſeven thunders had uttered, yet the angel pro- " ceeded to give a farther revelation of the provi- " dence of God, towards the world and his church " in general; and to confirm the truth and cer- " tainty of his revelation, he took his oath in the " moſt ſolemn manner; for lifting up his hand to " heaven, he ſware by the eternal God, the Crea- " tor of all things, that the time of the glorious " ſtate of the Church, though ſure to be accom- " pliſhed, according to God's promiſe, in its due " time, ſhould not be as yet. But in the next pe- " riod, or in the days of the voice of the ſeventh " angel, who was yet to ſound, the myſtery of " GOD, in his providence towards the Church, " ſhould be perfected; and then, as he had pro- " miſed in the prophetic Oracles, the glorious " ſtate of the Church ſhould be no longer deferred."

And to the ſame purpoſe ſpeaks Biſhop Newton: " Then the angel *lifted up his hand to heaven*, like " the angel in Daniel, xii. 7. *and ſware by him that* " *liveth for ever and ever*, the great Creator of all " things, (in the original) *that the time ſhall not be* " *yet*; but it ſhall be in the days of the Seventh " Trumpet, that *the myſtery of God ſhall be finiſhed* " and the glorious ſtate of his Church be perfected,

" agree-

" agreeably to the good things which he hath pro-
" mised to *his servants the prophets.* This is said for
" the consolation of Christians, that though the lit-
" tle book describes the calamities of the western
" church, yet they shall all have a happy period
" under the Seventh Trumpet."

I have nothing to add to the above explanations of those 6th and 7th verses: their meaning is plain and rational, so that he that runs may read.

The Sixth Trumpet has sounded long, from about the year 1281, to the present year 1793. But I am to shew, that it is now finished; and that *the second woe is past.*

There is an event mentioned in the verse immediately before my text, that points out the conclusion of the second woe, in as plain and direct a manner as possible; and such an event having taken place before our eyes, it is easy to see that the prophecy is now fulfilled.

Rev. xi. 13. " And the same hour was there a
" great earthquake, and the tenth part of the
" city fell, and in the earthquake were slain of men
" (as our translators render the words, but the ori-
" ginal words are literally, *names of men*) seven
" thousand: and the remnant were affrighted, and
" gave glory to the God of heaven."

By the great earthquake, we are to understand a great political shaking of some nation, whereby the government shall be overthrown and broken in pieces, as really as any part of the earth was ever broken and destroyed by a natural earthquake; and not only so, but this earthquake is to happen in one of the ten kingdoms, constituting the great hierarchy of *Rome*, which is often in this book stiled by way of eminence, *the great city*; and this earthquake is to be so violent, and to continue so long, that the tenth part of the city is to fall; that is, the king-

kingdom where this earthquake is to happen, will not only be broken in pieces itſelf, but will entirely fall off from Rome, and will no longer ſupport the papal government. And in this earthquake, which will be a ſudden and ſurprizing Revolution, different from all others, there will be ſlain of names of men ſeven thouſand; or, the whole number of the titles, or names of diſtinction will be deſtroyed; and all this will take place in a moſt ſudden and unexpected manner.

Now look at the Revolution, and overturning of the government in France, and ſee if this prophecy is not exactly fulfilled, and therein a full proof given that *the ſecond woe is paſt*, beyond all diſpute; and this epoch is therefore intereſting to all Chriſtians in the higheſt degree.

France is certainly a tenth part of the city or hierarchy of Rome, it is one of the ten horns of the beaſt, one of the ten kingdoms that gave its power and authority to the beaſt, which it has done in a moſt remarkable manner, from the days of Pepin, and his ſon Charlemagne, or Charles the Great, until the late Revolution. Theſe kings of France, were the very perſons who firſt made the Pope of Rome a temporal prince, by conquering Italy, ſubjecting the ſame to the Biſhop of Rome, and laying the keys at his feet. And France has all along been a ſteady and conſtant ſupporter of the papal religion, power and dignity; but it is now fallen, from that connexion, to riſe no more.

But it may be ſaid, that *England* itſelf might as well be called a tenth part of the City as *France*, and the ſame may be ſaid of *Ireland*, *Scotland*, *Sweden*, *Denmark;* for all theſe were horns of the papal beaſt, and all have fallen off from their attachment to Rome; how then is it to be known that the Revolution

lution in France is particularly intended in this paſſage?

I anſwer, If the Spirit of Truth had not given ſuch marks as diſtinguiſh the falling of France from the falling of all thoſe other powers, then we ſhould have been ſtill at a loſs. But it is to be obſerved, that in the earthquake or total Revolution that hath taken place in France, that there has been an entire ſlaughter of the *names of men*, that is of all *titles* of every kind. This is an event, however trifling in itſelf, that marks this period with the utmoſt preciſion and exactneſs. This has never taken place in any one of the kingdoms before that has fallen off from its connection with Rome; and conſequently proves the Revolution in France to be intended. And thus this event was predicted by the Spirit of prophecy, not for the importance of it conſidered in itſelf, but to mark it out preciſely as the concluſion of the ſecond woe, or the end of the ſounding of the ſixth Trumpet. And ſo this otherwiſe trifling occurrence, ſerves as a mark to the mariner, to let him know where he is, and what courſe to ſteer; and as ſeamen narrowly obſerve a noted certain ſea mark, not for the intrinſic worth and beauty of the object, but for an inconceivably higher purpoſe, to know where they are, and how to ſteer; ſo we may obſerve this event, as a certain mark or ſign of the cloſe of the ſixth angel ſounding his Trumpet; and ſo it becomes of the greateſt conſequence in this point of light.

Before this event took place, it was difficult to tell what was meant by *names of men*, which is the Greek expreſſion; our tranſlators could not ſee why ſuch a phraſe was uſed, and therefore rendered it ſimply *men*, nevertheleſs the true rendering is preſerved in the marginal reading, where it is *names of*

men.

men. But now the event having taken place, it is easy to see the exact correspondence between the prediction and its accomplishment.

It is a very remarkable circumstance, that *Peter Jurieu*, a famous French divine of Rotterdam, more than an hundred years ago, not only predicted the Revolution which has taken place, but understood the slaughter of the *names of men*, as a destruction, not of the persons of men, but of their names, or titles of distinction, and of the several religious orders, which he said would be abolished and destroyed, no more to be revived in France. And what is more extraordinary still, he predicted the time, when it would happen, allowing himself a latitude of ten years, from 1780 to 1790. This testimony of that worthy and venerable man, is almost sufficient of itself, to prove that what has lately taken place in France, precisely marks the conclusion of the second woe trumpet. But the matter is now so plain, as to be evident to every discerning eye.

There was also a religious discourse by Mr. Robert Fleming, printed in London in the first year of this century, 1701, in which are these words, Page 68. " So that there is good ground to hope, that about " the beginning of another such century, things may " again alter for the better; for I cannot but hope, " that some new mortification of the chief supporters " of Antichrist will then happen—And perhaps the " French Monarchy may begin to be considerably " humbled about that time; that whereas the present French King, takes the sun for his emblem, " and this for his motto, *Nec pluribus impar:* He may " at length, or rather his successors, and the monarchy itself, at least before the year 1794, be " forced to acknowledge, that in respect to neighbouring Potentates, he is *singulas impar.* But as

" to the expiration of this (fourth) vial, I do fear, " it will not be till the year 1794." Here he gives his reaſons.

Page 74. " I muſt tell you, I have nothing fur- " ther to add to what I have ſaid, as to time, but " as to the manner how this is to be done, our text " lays a foundation of ſome more diſtinct thoughts. " Therefore in the fourth and laſt place, we may " juſtly ſuppoſe, that the French Monarchy, after it " has ſcorched others, will itſelf conſume by doing " ſo; its fire, and that which is the fuel that main- " tains it, waſting inſenſibly, till it be exhauſted at " laſt, towards the end of this century."

This is alſo a very extraordinary prediction, coming ſo very near the time of the deſtruction of the French Monarchy; though I cannot agree with him, that it is done by the pouring out of the fourth vial; (none of which I apprehend to be yet poured out) but by the great political Earthquake, which has ſhaken that kingdom in pieces, and cauſed it to fall away from its connection with Rome; by which a tenth part of the City, or hierarchy of myſtical Babylon is ſunk down and deſtroyed, and the remainder will ſoon ſhare the ſame fate, by the pouring out of the vials; which awful diſpenſations will take place under the ſound of the Seventh Trumpet, which from this very time begins to ſound: and the Third woe will immediately commence.

It was ſaid, at the cloſe of the firſt woe, " One " woe is paſt, and behold there come two woes more " hereafter." Chap. ix. 12.

This ſuggeſted, that ſome time would intervene between the firſt woe of the Arabian locuſts, and the next of the Euphratean horſemen. But when the ſecond woe is paſt, it is ſaid, *Behold, the third woe cometh quickly.* There will be no intervening time

time between the ſecond and third woes; but upon the ceaſing of the *ſecond*, the third (which will bring the utter deſtruction of the prophetic beaſt) ſhall inſtantly begin.

Though this ſubject is ſo very plain, and though I have underſtood a long time, that this prophecy of the great earthquake, the fall of the tenth part of the City, and the ſlaying of the names of men, referred to what has happened in France; yet it never ſtruck me that the ſecond woe was actually paſt, till about three days ago, hearing the latter part of this eleventh chapter of the Revelations read, I was ſurprized to find immediately after the account of the earthquake, and what was brought about thereby, this ſolemn declaration made:—THE SECOND WOE IS PAST; and BEHOLD THE THIRD WOE COMETH QUICKLY. And then the Seventh Angel is immediately introduced as ſounding his trumpet; which is the moſt awful and important of all, and under which the third and great woe ſhall take place. A new and ſurprizing ſcene opened to my mind: I ſaw very plainly that the Sixth Trumpet was finiſhed, and the Seventh beginning to ſound; that the ſecond woe was paſt, and the third coming immediately; and I could not help being ſurprized that I had not obſerved it before, as the connection is ſo plain.

I regard the late events in France, therefore, as Signs of the Times, and they mark the cloſe of the preceding period with great exactneſs; and in this light their conſequence is very great: they ſhew us whereabouts we are, and tend to confirm the authority of the Scriptures, and eſpecially the book of the Revelation of St. John.

A new and very important period is now beginning to take place, under the ſound of the Seventh Trumpet, which will continue to ſound from this time, 'till after the perſonal appearance of JESUS, 'till all the ſeven vials of the wrath of God are poured out, and until *the kingdoms of this world are become the kingdoms of our Lord, and of his Chriſt.*

But great will be the woes and deſolations that will come upon the world before this happy event will take place. And for this reaſon, the ſeventh trumpet is properly denominated *a woe trumpet*, for the woes that will take place while it is ſounding, will be great beyond example, and terrible beyond deſcription.

Let us all flee for refuge to lay hold on the hope ſet before us, and pray with the Pſalmiſt, (Pſalm lvii. 1.) "Be merciful unto me, O God, be merciful unto me: for my ſoul truſteth in thee; yea, in the ſhadow of thy wings will I make my refuge, until theſe calamities be overpaſt."

The divine admonition to us ſeems at preſent to be as it is expreſſed in Iſaiah xxvi. 20, 21. "Come, my people, enter thou into thy chambers, and ſhut thy doors about thee: hide thyſelf, as it were, for a little moment, until the indignation be overpaſt. For behold, JEHOVAH cometh forth out of his place, to puniſh the inhabitants of the earth for their iniquity: The earth alſo ſhall diſcloſe her blood, and ſhall no more cover her ſlain."

The ſame great deſtruction is alſo ſpoken of by moſt of the Prophets, and the advice given by Zephaniah is now much in ſeaſon: "Gather yourſelves together, O nation not deſired: Before the decree bring forth, before the day paſs as the chaff, before the fierce anger of the Lord come upon you, before the day of JEHOVAH's anger come upon you."

"Seek

"Seek ye the Lord, all ye meek of the earth, "which have wrought his judgment; ſeek righte-"ouſneſs, ſeek meekneſs: It may be, ye ſhall be "hid in the day of JEHOVAH's anger."

"Therefore wait ye upon me, ſaith JEHOVAH, "until the day that I riſe up to the prey: for my "determination is to gather the nations, that I may "aſſemble the kingdoms, to pour upon them mine "indignation, even all my fierce anger; for all the "earth ſhall be devoured with the fire of my jealou-"ſy. For then will I turn to the people a pure "language, (or lip) that they may all call upon the "name of JEHOVAH, to ſerve him with one conſent "(or ſhoulder)." Zeph. ii. 1, 2, 3. Chap. iii. 8, 9. So that it is evident that very dreadful ſcenes will firſt take place, and then moſt glorious diſpenſations will ſucceed.

May the Lord prepare us for what is coming, and hide us from the evil, under the ſhadow of his wings, for his name's ſake. Amen.

DISCOURSE II.

Rev. xi. 15, 16, 17, 18.

AND THE SEVENTH ANGEL SOUNDED; AND THERE WERE GREAT VOICES IN HEAVEN, SAYING, THE KINGDOMS OF THIS WORLD ARE BECOME THE KINGDOMS OF OUR LORD, AND OF HIS CHRIST; AND HE SHALL REIGN FOR EVER AND EVER (OR TO THE AGES OF AGES). AND THE FOUR AND TWENTY ELDERS, WHO SAT BEFORE GOD ON THEIR SEATS, FELL UPON THEIR FACES AND WORSHIPPED GOD, SAYING, WE GIVE THEE THANKS, O LORD GOD ALMIGHTY, WHO ART, AND WAST, AND ART TO COME; BECAUSE THOU HAST TAKEN TO THEE THY GREAT POWER, AND HAST REIGNED. AND THE NATIONS WERE ANGRY, AND THY WRATH IS COME, AND THE TIME OF THE DEAD, THAT THEY SHOULD BE JUDGED, AND THAT THOU SHOULDEST GIVE REWARD UNTO THY SERVANTS THE PROPHETS, AND TO THE SAINTS, AND THEM THAT FEAR THY NAME, SMALL AND GREAT; AND SHOULDEST DESTROY THEM WHO DESTROY THE EARTH.

IN the ſermon which I had the honour to deliver in this place three weeks ago, I truſt it was made apparent that the ſecond woe was paſt, the ſounding of of the ſixth trumpet at an end, and the ſeventh beginning to ſound, and the third woe coming quickly. That diſcourſe treated almoſt entirely of things that are paſt; but this will be wholly filled with things that are to come.

I ſhall therefore directly proceed to ſet before you in their order, as plainly and as briefly as I can, the ſeveral events that will take place under the ſeventh trumpet, which is now beginning to ſound.

The ſeven vials of the wrath of God, or the ſeven laſt plagues, are all of them to be poured out under this trumpet, none of them being yet fulfilled. Biſhop Newton ſays, "Theſe ſeven laſt plagues "muſt neceſſarily fall under the ſeventh and laſt "trumpet, or the third and laſt woe trumpet; ſo "that as the ſeventh ſeal contained the ſeven trumpets, the ſeventh trumpet comprehends the ſeven "vials. Not only the concinnity of the prophecy "requires this order; for otherwiſe there would be "great confuſion, and the vials would interfere with "the trumpets, ſome falling under one trumpet, "and ſome under another: but, moreover, if theſe "ſeven laſt plagues, and the conſequent deſtruction "of Babylon be not the ſubject of the third woe, "the third woe is no where deſcribed particularly, "as are the two former woes. When four of the "ſeven trumpets had ſounded, it was declared, "(Chap. viii. 13.) *Woe, woe, woe to the inhabiters of "the earth, by reaſon of the other voices of the trumpets "of the three angels which are yet to ſound.* Accordingly, at the ſounding of the *fifth* trumpet (Chap. "ix. 1.) commences the woe of the Saracen or "Arabian locuſts; and in the concluſion is added, "(ver. 12.) *One woe is paſt, and behold there come two "woes more hereafter.* At the ſounding of the *ſixth* "trumpet (Chap. ix. 13.) begins the plague of the

"Euphra-

" Euphratean horſemen, or Turks; and in the concluſion is added, (Chap. xi. 14.) *The ſecond woe is paſt, and behold the third woe cometh quickly.* At the ſounding of the *ſeventh* trumpet, therefore, one would naturally expect the deſcription of the *third woe* to ſucceed; but there follows only a ſhort and ſummary account of the ſeventh trumpet, and of the joyful rather than of the woeful part of it. A general intimation indeed is given of God's taking *unto him his great power*, and *deſtroying them who deſtroy the earth*; but the particulars are reſerved for this place; (Chap. xvi. &c.) and if theſe laſt plagues coincide not with the laſt woe, there are other plagues and other woes after the laſt; and how can it be ſaid, that *the wrath of God is filled up in them*, if there are others beſides them? If then theſe ſeven laſt plagues ſynchronize with the ſeventh and laſt trumpet, they are all yet to come."

The account of the pouring out of the vials, contains in brief the awful judgments that ſhall come upon the enemies of our Lord, under the ſound of this ſeventh trumpet, and eſpecially upon the Church of Rome, and her adherents; and therefore I ſhall read the prophecy of the pouring out of thoſe vials, and make ſome brief remarks as I paſs along. But before I ſpeak particularly of the pouring out of the vials I would juſt call your attention to one expreſſion in the words that I firſt read, and which, being ſo plainly and remarkably fulfilled in our view, is fully ſufficient to prove, that the ſeventh trumpet hath already begun to ſound; and that is, *And the nations were angry:* this is a ſign of the times indeed, for was it ever ſeen before, that ſuch great and general preparations for war were made in Europe, as are making now! And as for the anger, wrath, and rage that are evident in all the European nations, which are now prepared and preparing for battle, the like has never been ſeen or heard of before. There ſeems ſuch terrible anger on all ſides, as though the *wrath* of God was *come*, and that the nations were gathering to pour out the vials of wrath upon each other. Even in this nation, where we may reaſonably expect the moſt coolneſs, and calm deliberation, it has been ſaid, that we ought to enter into the war, without conſidering in the leaſt what effect it might have upon our commerce, trade or wealth, and that if the nation ſhould be reduced, not only to the laſt guinea, but even to the laſt ſhilling, that ought to be no object at all. Yea more, ſome go ſo far as to pray, that an earthquake, or a volcano, or ſome other dreadful convulſion of nature ſhould ſwallow up or bury theſe Iſlands in the deep, with all their numerous inhabitants, multitudes of beaſts, and immenſe riches, rather than that even a change of politics ſhould take place here. With much more to the ſame purpoſe, which is ſufficient to prove, that even this cool and ſerious nation is very angry. What then is the ſtate of the other nations of Europe, whoſe paſſions are naturally more iraſcible and vindictive? their rage is indeſcribeable; as their ſpeeches, threatenings, writings and maniſeſtoes evidence, and above all their vigorous preparations for war, and their determination *to conquer or die*. I do not ſo much as enter into the matter in a political view, I mean to ſoar as far above that ſphere as the heavens are above the earth, and only ſpeak of theſe things as wonderful illuſtrations and fulfilments of prophecy.

The nations are now gathering on all ſides, like black clouds, charged with wind, hail, rain, thunder and fire, ready to diſcharge their baleful contents upon the aſtoniſhed world; and ſoon ſuch ſcenes will

will be opened to view, as ſhall terrify the ſenſes of all who ſhall ſee and hear.

I ſhall now paſs directly to the pouring out of the ſeven vials of God's wrath upon the earth. Rev. xvi. 1. " And I heard a great voice out of the tem-" ple, ſaying, to the ſeven angels, Go your ways, " and pour out the wrath of God upon the earth." On this verſe Biſhop Newton ſays, " In obedience " to the divine command, the ſeven angels come " forth *to pour out the vials of the wrath of God upon* " *the earth*; and as the trumpets were ſo many ſteps " and degrees of the ruin of the Roman empire, ſo " the vials are of the Roman Church. The one in " polity and government is the image of the other; " the one is compared to the ſyſtem of the world; " and hath her *earth* and *ſea*, and *rivers*, and *ſun* " as well as the other: and this is the reaſon of the " ſimilitude and reſemblance of the judgments in " both caſes. Some reſemblance too there is be-" tween theſe plagues and thoſe of Egypt. Rome " papal is diſtinguiſhed by the title of *ſpiritual Egypt*, " (Chap. xi. 8.) and reſembles Egypt in her puniſh-" ments as well as in her crimes, tyranny, idolatry, " and wickedneſs."

Verſe 2. " And the firſt went and poured out his " vial upon the earth; and there fell a noiſome and " grievous ſore upon the men who had the mark of " the beaſt, and upon them who worſhipped his " image."

This firſt vial is *poured out upon the earth*; and ſo the hail and fire of the firſt trumpet *were caſt upon the earth*, (ſee Chap. viii. 7.) whereby great deſtructions came upon the Roman empire: I apprehend that this firſt vial betokens great judgments to fall upon ſome inland part of the continent of Europe, and eſpecially upon that part of it that has been moſt noted for ſupporting the papal tyranny and ſuperſtition; and it ſtrikes me that this firſt vial will fall and ſpend itſelf upon *France* the *Netherlands*, and *Germany*, that vaſt inland country, the inhabitants of which have *had the mark of the beaſt* and have *worſhipped his image*, for ages paſt. Theſe powers are now aſſembling to deſtroy each other, or, in the language of prophecy, to pour out the contents of this *vial* of God's *wrath upon the earth*. The great trouble, pain and ſorrow now ready to fall upon that part of the globe, will be as terrible to the body politic, as the moſt *noiſome and grievous ſore* would be to the natural body of a man, or as the ſixth plague of Egypt, to which reference ſeems to be had, which was a *boil breaking forth with blains*, (Exod. ix. 10.) was to the inhabitants of that unhappy country.

This plague is to be particularly inflicted *upon the men who had the mark of the beaſt, and upon them who worſhipped his image*; which is to be underſtood of the others alſo where it is not expreſſed. Theſe wars will finally iſſue in the ruin of the papal power and authority in thoſe countries, and this will greatly grieve and vex the adherents of Antichriſt, and will be indeed a very *noiſome and grievous ſore* to them, which will pain them beyond expreſſion.

Verſe 3, 4, 5, 6, 7. " And the ſecond angel
" poured out his vial upon the ſea: and it became
" as the blood of a dead man; and every living ſoul
" died in the ſea. And the third angel poured out
" his vial upon the rivers and fountains of waters;
" and they became blood. And I heard the angel
" of the waters ſay, Thou art righteous O Lord,
" who art, and waſt, and ſhalt be, becauſe thou haſt
" judged thus: for they have ſhed the blood of
" ſaints and prophets, and thou haſt given them
" blood to drink; for they are worthy. And I

" heard

" heard another under the altar ſay, Even ſo, Lord " God Almighty, true and righteous are thy judg- " ments."

The ſecond vial is *poured out upon the ſea*, and the ſea becomes *as the blood of a dead man*, or as congealed blood: and in like manner under the ſecond trumpet, a burning mountain *was caſt into the ſea, and the third part of the ſea became blood*, &c. (Chap. viii. 8, &c.) The third vial is *poured out upon the rivers and fountains of water, and they became blood*: and in the ſame manner, under the third trumpet, the burning ſtar *fell upon the rivers and fountains of water*: (Chap. viii. 10.) There is a cloſe connection between theſe two vials; and the conſequences are ſimilar to the firſt plague of Egypt, when *the waters of Egypt*, and *their ſtreams*, and *their rivers*, and *their ponds*, and *all their pools of water became blood.* Exod. vii. 19.

Waters in the prophetical ſtile of this book, ſignify as explained (Chap. xvii. 15.) *Peoples and multitudes, and nations, and tongues*; ſeas and rivers of blood manifeſtly denote great ſlaughter and devaſtation; which will fall upon the nations which have been guilty of committing fornication with the Church of Rome, and have ſhed the blood of the ſaints like water, and have been drunken as it were therewith; theſe countries ſhall be made to drink blood in abundance, as a retaliation of the vaſt quantities of innocent and righteous blood which they have ſhed. I think by the *ſea, rivers and fountains of waters*, may be more particularly intended the maritime countries which are connected with Rome, and which have been guilty of idolatry, tyranny, cruelty, and eſpecially perſecution: and in this light it ſtrikes me that Spain, Portugal, and the iſlands and maritime parts of Italy, will drink very deep of theſe vials of wrath, which will fall heavy

upon

upon thoſe places, and upon all who have ſhed the blood of the martyrs under the popiſh influence. For God hath long ago judged the Pagan Empire of Rome, for the vaſt quantity of Chriſtian blood which it ſhed, and for which it was broken to pieces, overturned and deſtroyed: this took place under the four firſt trumpets; but now under the vials God will puniſh the Papal Empire more ſeverely than he did the Pagan, and it ſhall fall and riſe no more, as its tyranny and blood-thirſtineſs have more than equalled what were found in the empire while it was ſtill heathen. I ſhould be ſorry to be the meſſenger of heavy tidings to this land; but theſe iſlands were once under the Papal authority, and ſhed a conſiderable quantity of innocent and righteous blood, which cries aloud for vengeance, and makes me fear that even theſe lands may drink in ſome meaſure of theſe vials. God grant that the early renunciation of Rome, and the reformation that hath ſince taken place, with the piety, benevolence, and many virtues of this nation, may prevent the execution of the wrath which is threatened upon perſecutors, and upon their children, who approve of their deeds! I hope that none in theſe countries approve of thoſe wicked deeds of their forefathers. It was a prevailing opinion in the eaſt, that a particular angel preſided over the waters, as others did over other elements and parts of nature; and mention is made (Chap. xiv. 18.) of *the angel who had power over fire*. This angel of the waters celebrates the righteous judgments of God, in adapting and proportioning the puniſhments of the followers and worſhippers of the beaſt to their crimes; for no law can be more juſt and equitable than that they who have been guilty of *ſhedding the blood of the ſaints and prophets*, ſhould be puniſhed in the effuſion of their own blood.

" When

When the fifth ſeal was opened, St. John ſays, "I ſaw under the altar the ſouls of them that were "ſlain for the word of God, and for the teſtimony "which they held. And they cried with a loud "voice, ſaying, How long, O Lord, holy and true, "doſt thou not judge and avenge our blood on "them that dwell on the earth?" (Chap. vi. 9, 10.) So we find here, that when the vials are poured out upon the perſecuting nations and peoples, an *angel out of the altar*, as the repreſentative of all that have been ſacrificed by the papal perſecutions, declares his aſſent in the moſt ſolemn manner, *Even ſo, Lord God Almighty, true and righteous are thy judgments.* They who have read and impartially conſidered the authentic accounts of the oceans of blood that have been ſhed by thoſe nations that have been attached to the religion of Rome, will not be ſurpriſed to ſee very great deſolations come ſuddenly upon them: and as for the inhabitants of heaven, many of whom have ſuffered death by that blaſpheming and perſecuting power, they are called to rejoice aloud at its deſtruction. See Chap. xviii. 20. xix. 1, 2, 3, &c. and all muſt confeſs, that however dreadful theſe diſpenſations of deſtruction appear to us, God is juſt and true in all his judgments.

Ver. 8, 9, "And the fourth angel poured out "his vial upon the ſun: and power was given unto "him to ſcorch men with fire. And men were "ſcorched with great heat, and blaſphemed the "name of God, who hath power over theſe plagues: "and they repented not to give him glory."

As the fourth trumpet affected *the ſun* of the Roman weſtern empire, (Chap. viii. 12.) and cauſed a total change at Rome, by deſtroying the very name of Emperor; ſo I apprehend that the fourth vial will

will be poured out upon the Pope himſelf, who is the *ſun* of the papal empire, as the Roman emperor was of the empire of ancient Rome, and as Chriſt our Lord is the *ſun of righteouſneſs*, the *ſun* of his people; from whom their light, love, graces and fruitfulneſs proceed; he gives forth laws, and claims obedience. So does the Pope of Rome; and the people have long obeyed him, and conſidered him as the head and director of that kingdom; but the fourth vial ſhall be poured out upon him, and he will no longer reign, his power and his very name ſhall be deſtroyed. Nevertheleſs many of his former adherents will be ſo far from being converted to God by this evident token of his diſpleaſure againſt that cruel and perſecuting religion, that they will be full of rage and malice when they ſee their ſun deſtroyed. They will be inwardly tormented, and ſhall grievouſly complain; they ſhall, like the rebellious Jews, (Iſ. viii. 21.) "fret themſelves, and curſe their king, "and their God, and look upward." Look upward not to pray, but to blaſpheme; they ſhall not have the ſenſe or courage to repent, and forſake their idolatry and wickedneſs. But, on the contrary, they ſhall continue in rebellion, and blaſpheme God, as though he had forſaken the true Church, and ſuffered his promiſe to fail: for having this idea in their minds, that the Church of Rome is the only true Church, and the Pope its infallible head, when they ſee that he is fallen, and deſtroyed, they will be apt blaſphemouſly to conclude that Chriſt has failed to perform his promiſe, and that the gates of hell have prevailed againſt his Church. But why ſhould the Church of Rome imagine herſelf ſecure? Where is the Church of Jeruſalem, of Antioch, of Alexandria, of Conſtantinople, of Epheſus, &c.? Have they not gone to decay, and moſt of them ceased to exist? But the Christian religion, and the Christian Church, and the witnesses of Jesus have been found in every age.

Ver. 10, 11. "And the fifth angel poured out his "vial upon the seat of the beast; and his kingdom "was full of darkness, and they gnawed their tongues "for pain; and blasphemed the God of Heaven "because of their pains and their sores, and repent-"ed not of their deeds."

The fifth vial is to be *poured out upon the seat* or *throne of the beast, and his kingdom* becomes *full of darkness,* as Egypt did under her ninth plague (Exod. x. 21.) "This," (says Bishop Newton,) "is some great calamity which shall fall upon Rome, "and shall darken and confound the whole anti-"christian empire. But still the consequences of "this plague are much the same as those of the "foregoing one: for the sufferers, instead of *repent-"ing of their deeds,* are hardened like Pharaoh, and "still persist in their blasphemy and idolatry, and "obstinately withstand all attempts of reformation."

At the pouring out of the fifth vial I apprehend the city of Rome will be taken and sacked, and its destruction will then commence, which will be matter of great astonishment to the Romanists, to see not only the Pope fall, but the city of Rome itself taken, that city which they imagine to be as much God's peculiar possession, as ever the Jews believed Jerusalem to be so: and this event shall cause them to be filled with great astonishment, and shall make them *gnaw their tongues for pain,* and *blaspheme the God of Heaven,* as was observed before.

But though the destruction of Rome may begin by war, it shall be completed by fire, but whether fire from Heaven, as was upon Sodom and Gomorrah, or by a volcano breaking out in the city, I cannot ſay, but I conclude the latter. The adjacent countries are known to be of a ſulphureous and bituminous ſoil; and there have been even at Rome eruptions of ſubterraneous fires, which have conſumed ſeveral buildings; ſo that the fuel ſeemeth to be prepared, and waiteth only for the breath of the Lord to kindle it. And as ſure as the word of divine revelation is true, ſo ſure that famous city ſhall be utterly burnt with fire, and rendered for ever uninhabited and uninhabitable. For amongſt a great variety of expreſſions which the Lord makes uſe of to declare the total and utter deſtruction of the city on ſeven mountains, which in the Apoſtles time, ruled over the kings of the earth, which all, even Romaniſts themſelves, confeſs to be Rome, there are things mentioned which ſhall no more be found in her after her final overthrow, which are alone ſufficient to prove that the city ſhall remain for ever deſolate. "The voice of harpers, and mu-"ſicians, and of pipers, and trumpeters," (for which Rome is now, and has been ſo long famous) "ſhall be heard no more at all in thee."

2. "And no craftsman, of whatever craft he be, "ſhall be found any more in thee." So that there ſhall be no artificers, mechanicks, merchants, manufacturers, traders, or labourers there any more.

3. "And the ſound of a millſtone ſhall be heard "no more at all in thee." There ſhall be no food prepared there, not even bread, the ſtaff of life, and conſequently there can be no inhabitants.

4. "And the light of a candle ſhall ſhine no "more at all in thee." How famous Rome is at preſent, for a vaſt profuſion of lamps and candles! burning them both day and night in their churches, but the time ſhall certainly come when not one ſin-gle

gle candle ſhall be lighted there, and therefore certainly not one ſingle perſon ſhall lodge there.

5. " And the voice of the bridegroom and the " bride ſhall be heard no more at all in thee."

There ſhall be no *muſicians* for the entertainment of the rich and great; no more *tradeſmen* nor *artificers* to furniſh the conveniences of life, no more *ſervants* or *labourers* to grind at the mill, and ſupply the neceſſaries of life; nay, there ſhall be no more *lights*, no more *bridal ſongs*; the city ſhall never be again peopled by new marriages, but ſhall remain deſolate for ever. Her ſmoke ſhall riſe up *(eis tous aionas ton aionon)* for the ages of ages, or during the Millenium; ſhe ſhall be made as ſignal a monument of divine vengeance as Sodom and Gomorrah. This is the purpoſe of the Lord reſpecting Rome, who is myſtically called *Babylon* in this book, and ſhall be as certainly and utterly deſtroyed, as ancient Babylon of the Chaldeans was, and many of the prophetic expreſſions of the deſtruction of the one are applied to the other.

I have juſt touched upon the ſubject of the total deſtruction of Rome in the account of the fifth vial, as I ſhall not have time to ſpeak of it more particularly in this diſcourſe; though the deſcription and deſtruction of this city are matters of ſuch vaſt importance, that two whole chapters, beſides part of two others, are taken up therewith; and its final overthrow will be under the ſeventh vial, juſt after the coming of our Lord.

Ver. 12. " And the ſixth angel poured out his " vial upon the great river Euphrates; and the wa" ter thereof was dried up, that the way of the " kings of the eaſt might be prepared."

Here the ſcene appears to me to change, from the Papal to the Mahometan powers, and from Europe to Asia. As at the sound of the *sixth trumpet*, the Turks were *loosed* to *slay the third part of men*, so at the pouring out of the *sixth vial*, shall their power be weakened, diminished, and so far dried up, that they shall no longer be able either to hinder the Jews from returning to their own land, or to prevent the eastern nations which lie beyond them from receiving the gospel: both of which they hinder at present.

After the pouring out of the sixth vial, the Jews shall be gathered into their own country, and shall dwell for a little time in peace and safety, after which their enemies shall be gathered together against them, as foretold by Ezekiel, chap. xxxviii. xxxix. and by Zechariah, chap. xiv. These numerous foes of God and his people, shall be gathered in great numbers, and shall for a time prevail, but at the coming of the Lord, they shall be terrified and destroyed.

Ver. 13, 14. "And I saw three unclean spirits "like frogs come out of the mouth of the dragon, "and out of the mouth of the beast, and out of the "mouth of the false prophet: for they are the spi-"rits of devils working miracles, who go forth unto "the kings of the earth, and of the whole world, "to gather them to the battle of that great day of "God Almighty."

This great army appears to be composed of the Pagan, Mahometan and Papal powers united, gathered together by marvellous diabolical influence, with an intention to destroy and swallow up the Jews.

Ver. 15. "Behold I come as a thief. Blessed "is he that watcheth and keepeth his garments, lest "he walk naked, and they see his shame." Though this verse being here inserted, seems to disturb the

sense

ſenſe and break the connexion, it is introduced for a great purpoſe, and exactly in proper time. It not only ſhews that Chriſt will come ſuddenly and unexpectedly, and that thoſe are truly bleſſed who are prepared to meet him, who watch and pray, and walk in holy converſation and godlineſs; but it points out alſo the very time or ſeaſon when he will come, viz. between the pouring out of the ſixth and ſeventh vial, and when this great army ſhall be gathered together.

Ver. 16. "And he (or rather *they*, that is, the ſpirits of devils working miracles) "gathered them "together into a place called in the Hebrew tongue "*Armageddon*." That is *the mountain of deſtruction*. This mountain of deſtruction appears from other parts of the ſacred volume, to be a place not far from Jeruſalem; there theſe enemies ſhall fall and be deſtroyed, in the battle of that great day of God Almighty, when, as Zechariah ſays, "JEHOVAH, "ſhall go forth, and fight againſt thoſe nations, as "when he fought in the day of battle. And his "feet ſhall ſtand in that day upon the mount of "Olives, which is before Jeruſalem on the eaſt, "and the mount of Olives ſhall cleave in the midſt "thereof toward the eaſt, and toward the weſt, and "there ſhall be a very great valley; and half of the "mountain ſhall remove toward the north, and half "of it toward the ſouth." (Zech. xiv. 3, 4.) It ſhall be as evident as poſſible, when theſe words ſhall be fulfilled; the Lord will appear, the mount of Olives ſhall divide and remove, and this mighty hoſt ſhall be deſtroyed, and fall in a ſudden and awful manner. There will not then the leaſt ſhadow of a doubt remain. The ſame prophet informs us of the manner of their deſtruction, "Their fleſh ſhall "conſume away while they ſtand upon their feet,

" and their eyes ſhall conſume away in their holes; " and their tongue ſhall conſume away in their " mouth." Ver. 12.

So that it ſhall be ſeen to be the work of the Lord. But as I have treated of this ſubject at large in my Lectures on the Prophecies, I ſhall forbear, and proceed to the laſt vial.

Ver. 17. " And the ſeventh angel poured out his " vial into the air; and there came a great voice out " of the temple of Heaven, from the throne, ſay" ing, it is done."

The five firſt vials appear to be poured out on Europe, on the Papal powers; the ſixth upon the Turkiſh empire; but this ſeventh is *poured out into the air*, the ſeat of Satan's reſidence, who is emphatically ſtiled " the prince of the power of the air," (Epheſ. ii. 2.) and is repreſented as a principal actor in theſe latter ſcenes; ſo that this laſt period will not only complete the ruin of the kingdom of the beaſt, but will alſo ſhake the kingdom of Satan every where; and will prepare the way for the kingdom of Chriſt, by deſtroying his ſtubborn enemies, whether Pagans, Romaniſts, or Mahometans. The effects of this vial ſhall be very great and extenſive, far exceeding any of the others, or all of them put together.

Upon the pouring out of this vial a ſolemn proclamation is made *from the throne* of God himſelf, IT IS DONE; in the ſame ſenſe as the angel before affirmed (Chap. x. 7.) that " In the days of the ſeventh " trumpet the myſtery of God ſhould be finiſhed." Under the pouring out of this vial, which will take place, as before obſerved, after the coming of Chriſt, the third woe ſhall be finiſhed, and all the dreadful judgments ſhall end, and then immediately the glorious kingdom of Chriſt ſhall take place.

Some of the immediate effects of the seventh vial are mentioned in the following verses.

Ver. 18, 19. "And there were voices, and thun-"ders, and lightnings; and there was a great earth-"quake, such as was not since men were upon the "earth, so mighty an earthquake and so great. And "the great city was divided into three parts; and "the cities of the nations fell; and great Babylon "came into remembrance before God, to give unto "her the cup of the wine of the fierceness of his "wrath." These *voices, thunders, lightnings,* &c. portend very great calamities, and are the usual attendants of God, especially in his judgments. At the giving of the law at mount Sinai, "There were "thunders, and lightnings, and a thick cloud upon "the mount, and the voice of the trumpet exceed-"ing loud; And mount Sinai was altogether on a "smoke, because JEHOVAH descended upon it in "fire; and the smoke thereof ascended as the smoke "of a furnace, and the whole mount quaked "greatly." (Exod. xix. 16, 18.) So likewise in this very book of the Revelations, before the opening of the seven seals, (Chap. iv. 5,) we read, "And "out of the throne proceeded lightnings, and thun-"ders, and voices." So again before the sounding of the seven trumpets, (Chap. viii. 5.) "There "were voices, and thunders, and lightnings, and "an earthquake." And again at the opening of a new vision, we read (Chap. xi. 19.) "And the "temple of God was opened in heaven, and there "was seen in his temple the ark of his testament, "and there were lightnings, and voices, and thun-"derings, and an earthquake, and great hail." No wonder then that at the pouring out of this seventh vial, by which such great things are to be finished, that we should read of *voices,* and *thunderings* and

and *lightnings*, &c. *Great earthquakes*, in prophetic language, ſignify great changes and revolutions; and this, which ſhall take place under the ſeventh vial, ſhall be ſuch an one as men never felt nor experienced before, *ſuch as was not ſince men were upon the earth.* There is no doubt with me but that there will be great natural, as well as political earthquakes at the coming of our Lord, and before the full eſtabliſhment of his peaceable kingdom. But the mighty revolution that will take place when the kingdoms of this world will become the kingdoms of our Lord and of his Chriſt, may well be compared to a *great earthquake*, ſuch as never was known before, *ſo mighty an earthquake and ſo great.*

Great Babylon, or *Rome*, at this time will particularly come *in remembrance before God, to give unto her the cup of the wine of the fierceneſs of his wrath:* This is a ſubject of great conſequence, and therefore it is afterwards particularly reſumed, and a large account follows in the next chapters; but as I have already briefly noticed it, in ſpeaking of the fifth vial, I ſhall not ſay any thing farther upon it.

Ver. 20, 21. "And every iſland fled away, "and the mountains were not found. And there "fell upon men a great hail out of Heaven, every "ſtone about the weight of a talent: and men "blaſphemed God becauſe of the plague of the hail, "for the plague thereof was exceeding great."

It is ſaid in Chap. vi. 14, that "Every mountain "and iſland were moved out of their places;" which was intended to ſignify the ſubverſion of the Heathen religion, and its removal out of the Roman Empire, in the beginning of the fourth century; but in this place the expreſſions are much ſtronger, *the iſlands fly away, and the mountains are not found;* theſe words can import no leſs than the utter extirpation of all idolatry out of the whole world, where it hath reigned almoſt ever ſince the flood; for more than two thirds of mankind are at preſent mere ſtupid idolaters, and have been ſo in all ages to this day. But then all idols ſhall be utterly aboliſhed, and all idolatrous worſhip ſhall be deſtroyed, in order that all men that ſhall remain, may worſhip *one Lord*, who *ſhall be King over all the earth.*

Great hail often ſignifies great judgments, and when it is very large it is in itſelf a dreadful judgment. We read in Joſhua x. 11, that when the Children of Iſrael purſued the Amorites, " It came to paſs as they " fled from before Iſrael, and were in the going " down to Beth-horon, that JEHOVAH caſt down " great ſtones from Heaven upon them unto Azekah, and they died; they were more who died " with hailſtones, than they whom the Children of " Iſrael ſlew with the ſword."

And God threatens the great army of Gog, which ſhall be gathered to the battle of that great day, in this awful manner, " And I will plead againſt him " with peſtilence and with blood; and I will rain " upon him and upon his bands, and upon the many " peoples that are with him, an overflowing rain, " and great hailſtones, fire and brimſtone." Ezek. xxxviii. 22.

There hath frequently been very large hail, I have heard credible perſons ſay, that they have ſeen them as large as gooſe eggs. Diodorus, a grave hiſtorian, ſpeaks of hailſtones, which weighed a pound and more. Philoſtorgius mentions hail that weighed eight pounds; but theſe hailſtones are *about the weight of a talent*, or about a hundred pounds, probably a ſtrong figure to denote the greatneſs and ſeverity of theſe judgments, which ſhall take place at the pouring out of the ſeventh vial. But ſtill many men continue obſtinate, and *blaſpheme God because of the plague of the hail*: they remain incorrigible under the divine judgments, and muſt be deſtroyed before they will be reformed. This is the third time, in this chapter, that men are repreſented as *blaſpheming God*, *the name of God*, and *the God of Heaven*, under the moſt ſore and dreadful judgments that can be inflicted in this life, and therefore it is highly probable, as I have ſhewn in my Lectures, that by far the greater part of mankind will be deſtroyed, ſooner than ſubmit to the government of Chriſt. But this is no argument at all that he can never bring them to bow in a future ſtate, as ſome would ſuppoſe, becauſe they are hardened under theſe plagues, as Pharoah and moſt of the Egyptians were under the plagues of Egypt. For let it be conſidered, that all theſe plagues are inflicted upon men in this preſent life, and by which they are ſlain, ſo that none of theſe troubles can long continue here upon the moſt ſtubborn and rebellious; but God hath corrections after this life, which are far ſeverer than any that can be felt for a moment here, and they ſhall continue till all are ſubdued. So that none of this blaſpheming is ſpoken of as being the effect of God's puniſhments hereafter, but only in the preſent life, under thoſe plagues which ſhall come upon the earth and its inhabitants, before the kingdom of our Lord ſhall take place.

This chapter which I have now read, and endeavoured to explain, is indeed an awful chapter, and contains a ſketch in miniature of the third and laſt woe, which ſhall take place under the ſounding of this ſeventh trumpet, which I apprehend is now begun. I might ſay much more upon the dreadful judgments that ſhall come upon the rebellious; but there are a number of other matters in the words of my text, which demand our consideration, and which are joyful subjects, of the greatest importance.

Under the seventh trumpet our glorious Saviour will personally appear; I have already observed, that he will come between the time of the sixth and seventh vial; all these awful dispensations that are taking place are solemn preparations for that event; and therefore our Lord charges us when we hear of wars and rumours of wars, to *see* that we *be not troubled; for all these things must come to pass.* St. Matt. xxiv. 6. St. Mark xiii. 7. St. Luke xxi. 9. And he points out the signs of his coming in the following manner, "And there shall be signs in the sun, and "in the moon, and in the stars; and upon the earth "distress of nations, with perplexity, the sea and "the waves roaring; mens hearts failing them for "fear, and for looking after those things which are "coming on the earth; for the powers of Heaven "shall be shaken. And then shall they see the Son "of Man coming in a cloud, with power and great "glory. And when these things begin to come to "pass, then look up, and lift up your heads; for "your redemption draweth nigh." St. Luke xxi. 25, 26, 27, 28. The coming of our Saviour in glory, is such a joyful event in itself, and will be followed by so many glorious consequences, that it is almost impossible for a true Christian to think of it without exultation. And this will actually take place under the sound of the seventh trumpet.

Another event that stands connected with the sounding of the seventh trumpet, is the *first resurrection*, or, the resurrection of the just, for the time of the sounding of the seventh trumpet is *the time of the dead, that they should be judged*, and consequently they must be raised, and we are assured that when Christ shall come, he shall come with all his saints,

 1. Thess.

1. Theſſ. iii. 13. "For if we believe that Jeſus died "and roſe again, even ſo them alſo who ſleep in "Jeſus, will God bring with him. For this we "ſay unto you by the word of the Lord, that we "who are alive and remain unto the coming of the "Lord, ſhall not prevent them who are aſleep. "For the Lord himſelf ſhall deſcend from Heaven "with a ſhout, and with the voice of the archangel, "and with the trump of God: and the dead in "Chriſt ſhall riſe firſt. Then we who are alive "and remain, ſhall be caught up with them in the "clouds, to meet the Lord in the air: and ſo ſhall "we ever be with the Lord." 1. Theſſ. iv. 14. 15, 16, 17.

"When Chriſt, who is our life ſhall appear, "then ſhall ye alſo appear with him in glory." Col. iii. 4. Thus this great event of the reſurrection of the dead ſaints, and the changing of thoſe who are prepared for it, who ſhall be found alive, are ſome of thoſe grand events which ſhall take place at the coming of our Lord, and conſequently under the ſounding of the preſent ſeventh trumpet.

The giving rewards to the juſt, is another of thoſe glorious events which ſhall come to paſs under the ſound of this trumpet. Thanks are aſcribed to God that the time is come, *that thou ſhouldeſt give reward unto thy ſervants the prophets, and to the ſaints, and them that fear thy name, ſmall and great.* We have great reaſon to rejoice, that the rewards of the Millenium are not confined to the prophets, apoſtles, martyrs, and firſt ſaints, but extend to all that fear or revere the name of the Lord, both ſmall and great. If none were mentioned but firſt rate characters, it would be diſcouraging to the weak, feeble, and tempted Chriſtians, who yet fear the Lord, and endeavour to walk in his ways with ſincere hearts: but

but for the encouragement of ſuch, all that fear the Lord, both ſmall and great, are included in the promiſed reward. When St. Paul exulted in view of the celeſtial crown, he did not confine it to himſelf alone, nor to the Apoſtles, nor to the martyrs, "I have fought, (ſays he,) a good fight. I have "finiſhed my courſe, I have kept the faith; Hence-"forth there is laid up for me a crown of righteouſ-"neſs, which the Lord the righteous Judge ſhall "give me at that day: and not unto *me only*, but "unto all them alſo that love his appearing." 2 Tim. iv. 7, 8. The leaſt true lover of Jeſus is here included, ſo that none have reaſon to be diſcouraged.

St. James, ſays, "Bleſſed is the man that en-"dureth temptation; for when he is tried, he ſhall "receive a crown of life, which the Lord hath "promiſed to them that love him." James i. 12. That glorious paſſage in the twentieth chapter of this book of Revelations, which deſcribes thoſe who ſhall have a part in the firſt reſurrection, though it firſt mentions the martyrs, includes all the faithful worſhippers of God, and ſuch who had not worſhipped the beaſt, &c. "And I ſaw thrones, and they "ſat upon them, and judgment was given unto "them: and I ſaw the ſouls of them that were be-"headed for the witneſs of Jeſus, and for the word "of God, and who had not worſhipped the beaſt, "neither his image, neither had received his mark "upon their foreheads, or in their hands; and "they lived and reigned with Chriſt a thouſand "years. But the reſt of the dead lived not again "until the thouſand years were finiſhed. This is "the firſt reſurrection. Bleſſed and holy is he that "hath part in the firſt reſurrection: on ſuch the "ſecond death hath no power, but they ſhall be "priests of God and of Christ, and shall reign with "him a thousand years." Rev. xx. 4, 5, 6. It is plain that all whom God brings with him shall have a part in the first resurrection, and we have already seen that those *who sleep in Jesus, will God bring with him.* And the Lord, by the Prophet Malachi, after speaking of the dreadful day that shall consume the wicked doers, adds the following words for the comfort of his people, "But unto you that fear my "name, shall the sun of righteousness arise with "healing in his wings; and ye shall go forth and "grow up as calves of the stall." Mal. iv. 2.

"Then they that feared JEHOVAH, spake often "one to another, and JEHOVAH hearkened, and "heard it, and a book of remembrance was written "before him for them that feared JEHOVAH, and "that thought upon his name. And they shall be "mine, saith JEHOVAH of Hosts, in that day when "I make up my jewels, and I will spare them as a "man spareth his own son that serveth him." Mal. ii. 16, 17. Here you see are gracious promises to all that fear the Lord, and that think on his name; and no man deserves so much as the name of a Christian, who doth not do so. Moreover the blessed Saviour secures all who believe and trust in him from the second death, which I take to be implied in these words, "I am the resurrection and "the life; he that believeth in me, though he were "dead, yet shall he live: And whosoever liveth "and believeth in me shall never die." St. John xi. 25, 26.

"Verily, verily I say unto you, He that heareth "my word, and believeth on him that sent me, "hath everlasting life, and shall not come into "condemnation; but is passed from death unto "life," St. John v. 24.

"Verily, verily I ſay unto you, He that be-
"lieveth on me hath everlaſting life." St. John vi. 47.

"Verily, verily I ſay unto you, if a man keep
"my ſaying, he ſhall never ſee death." St. John viii. 51.

Theſe are all very encouraging paſſages of Scripture, and point out who ſhall obtain the reward in ſuch a manner, as not to diſcourage any who truly fear God, believe in Jeſus, and obey the Goſpel.

What are thoſe rewards which God ſhall give to the prophets, ſaints, and to thoſe who fear his name, both ſmall and great? Theſe I muſt but barely mention, and ſhall confine myſelf to this book of the Revelations.

1. They *ſhall not be hurt of the ſecond death*; Rev. ii. 11.

2. They ſhall have a *part in the firſt reſurrection*; Chap. xx. 6.

3. They ſhall *eat of the tree of life, which is in the midſt of the Paradiſe of God*; Chap. ii. 7.

4. They ſhall *eat of the hidden manna*; Ver. 17.

5. They *ſhall be clothed in white raiment*; Chap. iii. 5.

6. They ſhall have *a white ſtone* given to them; *and in the ſtone a new name written, which no man knoweth ſaving he that receiveth it.* Chap. ii. 17. which implies an entire freedom from all condemnation.

7. Their names ſhall not be blotted *out of the book of life*; Chap. iii. 5.

8. Their names ſhall be confeſſed with honour by our Lord Jeſus, before his *Father, and before his Angels*: Ver. 5.

9. They *ſhall walk with* Chriſt *in white*, being judged *worthy* of ſo great an honour: Ver. 4.

10. Chriſt

10. Chriſt will write upon them three great and honourable names; thus expreſſed by himſelf, *The name of my God, and the name of the city of my God, New Jeruſalem, which cometh down out of Heaven from my God: and my new name:* ſays the bleſſed Jeſus: Ver. 12.

11. They ſhall have *power over the nations; and they ſhall rule them with a rod of iron*, to ſubdue *them, even* as Chriſt *received* of his *Father:* Chap. ii. 26, 27.

12. Each of them ſhall have *a crown of life;* Ver. 10.

13. *They ſhall be prieſts of God and of Chriſt, and ſhall reign with him a thouſand years:* Chap. xx. 6.

14. They ſhall *ſit with* Chriſt *in his throne, even as he overcame*, and is *ſet down with the Father in his throne:* Chap. iii. 21.

15. Chriſt *will make* them *pillars in the temple of God*, and they *ſhall go no more out:* Ver. 12.

16. He will give them *the morning ſtar:* Chap. ii. 28.

17. *They ſhall ſee his face; and his name ſhall be in their foreheads:* Chap. xxii. 4.

18. They ſhall *have a right to the tree of life*, and ſhall *enter in through the gates into the city*, the New Jeruſalem. Ver. 14.

19. They *ſhall inherit all things;* Chap. xxi. 7.

20. *They ſhall reign for ever and ever;* in the new earth. Chap. xxii. 5.

Theſe glorious rewards are ſufficient to animate the hopes of all that fear the name of the Lord, both ſmall and great. But I muſt not enlarge.

The great event of all, which is contained in the words of my text, and which is celebrated in the praiſes of the elders, is the kingdom of Chriſt on

earth,

earth, and his dominion over the kingdoms of this world.

I have already spoken of his victory over Antichrist, and some of the methods whereby he shall destroy his stubborn and rebellious foes, who *will not have him to reign over them.* When this is effected, his kingdom and government shall take place universally through the globe, and prevail over all.

There is one method which he will take to bring all nations to submit to his government, which is the most effectual that could possibly be devised; and that is, that there shall be no rain upon the countries of those people who refuse to do homage to him; for it is certain that this is one of the most irresistible means in nature, and will certainly be effectual in all those lands which depend upon the showers of Heaven for their food; and there is an exception made respecting those countries which have no dependence upon rain for their fruitfulness, and for the subduing of which another judgment is appointed. Though this is prophesied of but once, yet it is a most plain and positive prediction, and expressed in clear and determinate language. See Zech. xiv. 16, 17, 18, 19. "And it shall come "to pass, that every one that is left of all the "nations which came against Jerusalem, shall even "go up from year to year to worship the King, "Jehovah of Hosts, and to keep the feast of "tabernacles. And it shall be, that whoso will not "come up of all the families of the earth unto "Jerusalem, to worship the King, Jehovah of "Hosts, even UPON THEM SHALL BE NO RAIN. "And if the family of Egypt go not up, and come "not, that have no rain; there shall be the plague "wherewith Jehovah will smite the heathen that

"come not up to keep the feaſt of tabernacles.
" This ſhall be the puniſhment of Egypt, and the
" puniſhment of all nations that come not up to keep
" the feaſt of tabernacles."

The matter is exceeding plain, and it is impoſſible to ſpiritualize it away; for it is not the witholding of the ſpiritual rain of righteouſneſs and grace, that would ever make the nations ſubmit to Jeſus, but the witholding of the natural rain will ſoon bring them down. Beſides, would any perſon aſſert that Egypt, that was once famous for chriſtianity, never had any ſpiritual rain? this would be abſurd to the laſt degree. Let the words ſtand as they are, and they make good ſenſe, but alter them any way, and they become nonſenſe. If Egypt, and other African countries that have no rain, refuſe to ſubmit, the inhabitants ſhall be cut off by a ſudden and terrible plague, ſimilar to what is mentioned, Zech. xiv. 12. And all other countries that refuſe to bow ſhall be abſolutely deprived of rain until they ſubmit.

It is very eaſy to ſee that in a very ſhort time all nations ſhall be brought to yield obedience to him; and *the kingdoms of this world* ſhall *become the kingdoms of our Lord and of his Chriſt; and he ſhall reign, eis tous aionas ton aionon*; which our tranſlators have tranſlated, *for ever and ever*, but which appears in (Chap. xx. 2, 3, 4, 5, 6, 7,) to be only *a thouſand years*, and is ſix times limited to that period. So that here the words which are uſed imply *hidden duration*, or *ages of ages*, without ſpecifying the exact length of the periods: but in Chap. xx. the time is made known with great exactneſs. It is true that Chriſt ſhall reign much more than a thouſand years in all, *for he ſhall reign till he hath put all enemies under his feet*: 1 Cor. xv. 25; but his reign over the *kingdoms of this world*, before the ſecond reſurrection, the ge-

neral

neral judgment and the conflagration," shall be a thousand years. And this the period spoken of in the words of my text. There is nothing in this view of the kingdom of Christ, that has any tendency to give umbrage or dissatisfaction to the present monarchs, kings, rulers, or governors of the earth, for though all the kingdoms of the world shall become the Lord's, and his Christ's, yet this is no encouragement for any usurpers to rise and seize upon them, under a pretence of their being the Lord's people, and that they are going to take possession of the kingdoms for him; for Christ himself will come in person, to take the kingdoms of this world under his government, so that this part of my text will not be accomplished till after his appearing in glory, and the first resurrection has taken place.

But although there is nothing said here which can reasonably give the smallest offence to the kings of the earth, yet if I had the honour of addressing them all at this time, I would press earnestly upon them the advice which David gave them so long ago. "Be wise now, therefore, O ye kings! "be instructed, ye judges of the earth! Serve "JEHOVAH with fear, and rejoice with trembling, "kiss the Son, lest he be angry, and ye perish from "the way, when his wrath is kindled but a little. "Blessed are all they that put their trust in him." Psalm ii. 10, 11, 12.

Christ our Saviour is the rightful heir to all the kingdoms of the world, and he will at length obtain possession of his right; "yea, all kings shall fall "down before him: all nations shall serve him." Psalm lxxii. 11.

He will be just such an absolute monarch as all good men would wish should govern the world, and reign over mankind.

1. He will possess infinite *wisdom*, will know all the affairs of his empire, without any possibility of being deceived; his laws will be a compleat system of rectitude and harmony, and all his rules shall be such models of perfection, that he shall never have occasion to make any alteration in them.

2. His *power* shall be as great as his wisdom, so that he shall reign absolute every where, and make his laws universally obeyed; and during the whole time of the Millenium all mankind shall serve him, and glorify his name.

3. His *goodness* shall equal his power, and his government shall be the greatest blessing to mankind that ever they enjoyed, or even formed an idea of; it being calculated to produce the greatest sum of happiness that their situation will then admit of.

4. He shall not die, and leave his empire to a successor; and consequently there shall be no possibility of his government degenerating into tyranny, as has often been the case with good governments.

I will now as a close of this discourse, just mention the blessings of the Millenium, or the personal kingdom of our Lord upon the earth. And I must but just mention them, and refer you to the second volume of my Lectures on the Prophecies, for a full account and description of them. And therefore I shall mention them in the same order in which I have treated of them there.

1. The kingdom or goverment of Christ shall be absolutely universal, and shall extend over the whole earth: all nations shall know his name, and shall serve and obey him. "He shall have dominion "also from sea to sea, and from the river unto the "ends of the earth. They that dwell in the wil-"derness shall bow before him; and his enemies shall "lick the dust. The kings of Tarshish and of the "isles

"isles shall bring presents, Sheba and Seba shall "offer gifts. Yea, all kings shall fall down before "him; all nations shall serve him." Psalm lxxii. 8, 9, 10, 11.

2. His government shall be *just*, *equitable*, *righteous*, friendly to mankind, especially to the poor and needy. There shall be no oppression, injustice, or defrauding amongst mankind during the time of his reign. As his laws shall be *just*, so his government "shall be as the light of the morning when the sun "riseth, even a morning without clouds; as the "tender grass springing out of the earth by clear "shining after rain." 2 Sam. xxiii. 4. "He shall "judge the poor of the people, he shall save the "children of the needy, and shall break in pieces "the oppressor. For he shall deliver the needy when "he crieth: the poor also, and him that hath no "helper. He shall spare the poor and needy, and "shall save the souls of the needy. He shall re-"deem their soul from deceit and violence: and "precious shall their blood be in his sight." Psal. lxxii. 4, 12, 13, 14.

3. Another blessing that shall take place under the Messiah's government, shall be universal and constant *peace*, during the whole period of his reign. This is prophesied of in the most express terms, both by Isaiah, Chap. ii. and Micah, Chap. iv. in these words: "And he shall judge among the na-"tions, and shall rebuke many people: and they shall "beat their swords into plow-shares, and their "spears into pruning hooks: nation shall not lift up "sword against nation, neither shall they learn war "any more." Isaiah ii. 4.

"And he shall judge among many people, and "rebuke strong nations afar off; and they shall beat "their swords into plow-shares, and their spears

" into pruning hooks, (or ſcythes) nation ſhall not
" lift up a ſword againſt nation, neither ſhall they
" learn war any more. But they ſhall ſit every man
" under his vine and under his fig-tree; and none
" ſhall make them afraid: for the mouth of JEHO-
" VAH hath ſpoken it." Micah iv. 3, 4.

" The mountains ſhall bring peace to the people,
" and the little hills by righteouſneſs. In his days
" ſhall the righteous flouriſh; and abundance of
" peace ſo long as the moon endureth." Pſal. lxxii.
3, 7.

" And he ſhall ſpeak peace unto the Heathen;
" and his dominion ſhall be from ſea to ſea, and
" from the river even to the ends of the earth."
" Zech. ix. 10.

" In that day, ſaith JEHOVAH of Hoſts, ſhall ye
" call every man his neighbour under the vine, and
" under the fig-tree." Chap. iii. 10.

Thus it is evident, that war ſhall be no more known in that happy time, nor ſhall it be taught as an art, nor ſhall weapons of war be made, nor any thing tending thereto be encouraged, but on the contrary. This plainly ſhews that the time has never yet been; for to this day wars have been made, and preparations carried on: but then it ſhall be ſo no more.

4. In the time of the Millenium it appears from prophecy, that all enmity ſhall be deſtroyed from among the animals, and they ſhall be brought nearly into the ſtate they were in when they were firſt created. " The wolf alſo ſhall dwell with the lamb, and
" the leopard ſhall lie down with the kid; and the
" calf, and the young lion, and the fatling together,
" and a little child ſhall lead them. And the cow
" and the bear ſhall feed, their young ones ſhall lie
" down together: and the lion ſhall eat ſtraw like

" the

"the ox. And the ſucking child ſhall play on the
"hole of the aſp, and the weaned child ſhall put
"his hand on the cockatrice den. They ſhall not
"hurt nor deſtroy in all my holy mountain: for
"the earth ſhall be full of the knowledge of JEHO-
"VAH, as the waters cover the ſea." Iſaiah xi. 6,
7, 8, 9.

"The wolf and the lamb ſhall feed together, and
"the lion ſhall eat ſtraw like the bullock; and duſt
"ſhall be the ſerpents meat. They ſhall not hurt
"nor deſtroy in all my holy mountain ſaith JEHO-
VAH." Chap. lxv. 25.

5. Another bleſſing that ſhall take place and continue during the Millenium is *plenty*; the curſe ſhall be taken from the earth, and it ſhall yield immenſe increaſe with but very little labour. "Then ſhall "the earth yield her increaſe; and God, even our "own God ſhall bleſs us." Pſal. lxvii. 6. God ſays, "And I will cauſe the ſhower to come down in "his ſeaſon, there ſhall be ſhowers of bleſſing: "And the tree of the field ſhall yield her fruit, and "the earth ſhall yield her fruit, and the earth ſhall "yield her increaſe, and they (the people) ſhall be "ſafe in their land. And I will raiſe up for them a "plant of renown, and they ſhall be no more con-"ſumed with hunger in the land." Ezek. xxxiv. 26, 27, 29. Whether this plant of renown is the bread fruit-tree, (which government has taken ſuch pains to tranſplant from the iſland of Otaheite, to the Weſt Indies) or any other plant that ſhall be raiſed for the ſame purpoſe, I ſhall not pretend abſolutely to determine; but it is very certain that the fear of famine ſhall be wholly removed in that time. "And "I will call for the corn, and will increaſe it, and "will lay no famine upon you. And I will multi-"ply the fruit of the tree, and the increaſe of the

" field, that ye ſhall recieve no more reproach of " famine." Ezek. xxxvi. 29, 30.

The earth ſhall be filled with *plenty;* as well as *peace,* and neither war, famine, peſtilence, nor the terrible fierceneſs of wild beaſts ſhall annoy, hurt, deſtroy or even terrify the inhabitants of the earth in thoſe bleſſed days.

6. I conſider it as highly probable, if not abſolutely certain, that in the time of the Millenium, women ſhall bring forth the fruit of the womb without danger, and with little or no pain; being delivered from the curſe pronounced at the fall. " They ſhall not labour in vain, nor bring forth " for trouble: for they are the ſeed of the bleſſed " of JEHOVAH; and their offspring with them." Iſaiah lxv. 23.

7. And as the danger and pain of child bearing ſhall be in a great meaſure, if not wholly removed, ſo they ſhall not have that ſorrow which is now ſo common of being deprived of their children in their infancy. " There ſhall be no more thence an infant " of days, nor an old man that hath not filled his " his days: for the child ſhall die an hundred years " old; but the ſinner being an hundred years old " ſhall be accurſed." Iſaiah lxv. 20.

Or as Biſhop Lowth renders the paſſage,

" No more ſhall be there an infant ſhort lived;
" Nor an old man who hath not fulfilled his days;
" For he that dieth at an hundred years ſhall die a
" boy;
" And the ſinner that dieth at an hundred years ſhall
" be deemed accurſed."

So that it is evident that no infants ſhall die.

8. It

8. It is plain from the ſame words, and from the following verſes, that the ancient longevity of men before the flood ſhall be reſtored.

" And they ſhall build houſes, and ſhall inhabit
" them;
" And they ſhall plant vineyards, and ſhall eat the
" fruit thereof.
" They ſhall not build, and another inhabit;
" They ſhall not plant, and another eat.
" For as the days of a tree ſhall be the days of my
" people;
" And they ſhall wear out the works of their own
" hands.
" My choſen ſhall not labour in vain;
" Neither ſhall they generate a ſhort lived race;
" For they ſhall be a ſeed bleſſed of JEHOVAH;
" They, and their offſpring with them."

Ver. 21, 22, 23. *Lowth's tranſlation.*

9. In the Millenium, or during the thouſand years of the reign of Chriſt, the earth will anſwer the great purpoſe for which it was made; for God " created " it not in vain, he formed it to be inhabited." Iſaiah xlv. 18. but it hath never ſince the flood been a quarter populated, nor a tenth part of it cultivated; and a great part of it at preſent cannot be inhabited and tilled, becauſe of its barrenneſs in conſequence of the curſe; but when the moſt barren deſarts ſhall become fruitful fields, and the curſe ſhall be removed, and the earth ſhall yield its increaſe: and when wars, famines, peſtilences, plagues and deſolations ſhall be no more, and no children ſhall die in their infancy, the world ſhall ſoon become very populous; and according to the calculation which I have made in my Lectures, more than five hunderd times the number may be born during the

time of the Millenium, than have been born ſince the creation, even allowing ſixty perſons to have been born every minute from that time to the end of ſix thouſand years.

So that our Lord may be able with truth to ſay, that there are more happy under his government at once in the time of his kingdom on earth, than ever ſin and death tyrannized over, put all together from the beginning of time.

10. In the time of our Saviour's reign on earth, the world ſhall not only be full of people, living happily in *peace*, *health*, and *plenty*, under the moſt excellent government, but they ſhall all know, fear, love, ſerve, and adore the Lord, with all their hearts. The knowledge of God ſhall be univerſal; for thus his word declares. "For the earth ſhall be "filled with the knowledge of the glory of JEHO-"VAH, as the waters cover the ſea." (Hab. ii. 14.) "As truly as I live, all the earth ſhall be filled with "the glory of JEHOVAH. Numbers xiv. 21.

"For, from the riſing of the ſun to the going "down of the ſame, my name ſhall be great among "the Gentiles; and in every place incenſe ſhall be "offered unto my name, and a pure offering: for "my name ſhall be great among the Heathen, "ſaith JEHOVAH of Hoſts." Mal. i. 11.

"For the earth ſhall be full of the knowledge "of JEHOVAH, as the waters cover the ſea." Iſai. xi. 9.

"They ſhall teach no more every man his "neighbour, and every man his brother, ſaying, "Know JEHOVAH; for all ſhall know me, from "the leaſt of them unto the greateſt of them, ſaith "JEHOVAH; for I will forgive their iniquity, "and remember their ſin no more." Jer. xxxi. 34.

These

These paſſages ſufficiently prove that the knowledge of God ſhall be univerſal at that time. God will write his laws upon the hearts of all men, and they ſhall ſerve him willingly, with the higheſt delight and ſatisfaction. Then ſhall it be far more difficult to find vice upon earth than it is now to find virtue; as I truſt I have made evident in my Lectures, to which I refer you.

11. In thoſe bleſſed times there ſhall be no differences of ſentiment: all ſhall be harmony and love: no contradiction in the public inſtructions: all miniſters ſhall agree, in principle and practice, in faith and worſhip. "Thy watchmen ſhall lift "up the voice; with the voice together ſhall they "ſing: for they ſhall ſee eye to eye, when JE- "HOVAH ſhall bring again Zion." Iſaiah lii. 8. So that there ſhall be no diviſion among the teachers; but they ſhall *be perfectly joined together in the ſame mind, and in the ſame judgment.* 1 Cor. i. 10.

12. Then ſhall our Saviour's prayer for unity in his Church be anſwered and accompliſhed, and the glorious conſequences ſhall follow. "That they "(who believe in me) all may be one; as thou "Father art in me, and I in thee, that they alſo "may be one in us; that the world may believe "that thou haſt ſent me.—That they may be one, "even as we are one. I in them, and thou in me, "that they may be made perfect in one, and that "the world may know that thou haſt ſent me." St. John xvii. 21, 22, 23. When this perfect unity takes place among believers, the converſion of the whole world will ſoon follow. Theſe are ſome of the great and glorious bleſſings that will take place under the government of the Lord, in the time of the Millenium; and which will render his kingdom

worthy

worthy of being the ſubject of the higheſt exultation and praiſe of all the hoſts of Heaven, who will ſay as in the words of my text, with which I ſhall conclude, "WE GIVE THEE THANKS, O LORD, "GOD, ALMIGHTY, WHO ART, AND WAST, AND "ART TO COME; BECAUSE THOU HAST TAKEN "TO THEE THY GREAT POWER, AND HAST "REIGNED."

www.ingramcontent.com/pod-product-compliance
Lightning Source LLC
Chambersburg PA
CBHW020226090426
42735CB00010B/1602
9783337102616